W9-BDA-002

☆

GROVER CLEVELAND

☆

B
6

GROVER CLEVELAND

by

Edwin P. Hoyt

REILLY & LEE CO.
Chicago 1962

WINGATE COLLEGE LIBRARY
WINGATE, N. C.

Illustrations reproduced through the courtesy
of the New York Historical Society

COPYRIGHT 1962 BY EDWIN P. HOYT
MANUFACTURED IN THE UNITED STATES OF AMERICA
LIBRARY OF CONGRESS CARD NO. 62-7506

for HELGA,
        so that she may understand the true
sources of strength and greatness

22286

✩✩ Contents

☆

GROVER CLEVELAND

☆

✭ the minister's son

IT SEEMS ODD that among the thirty-five men who have been elected President of the United States one of the strongest men of all should also be among the least known of our Presidents, but that is the truth regarding Grover Cleveland, who served as twenty-second and twenty-fourth President.

Cleveland's career is remarkable, first of all, because he is the only man to have been elected President twice, but not consecutively. He was first elected President in 1884, then he was defeated by Benjamin Harrison in 1888. In 1892, he turned the tables and defeated Harrison. It was notable that he was able to win again after a defeat, and equally notable that he was able to secure the nomination of his own Democratic party after such an important defeat.

Cleveland should be famous, too, because he entered the Presidency after only three years of prominence in politics. It is hard to imagine that a man could be a private citizen— a lawyer—at one moment, and then be catapulted into the Presidency almost the next moment, yet that is exactly what happened to Cleveland. He was living quietly in Buffalo, New York, in 1880, as a prosperous lawyer in a booming, busy Great Lakes port city. He had relatively little interest in politics, and while he had served one term as sheriff, and had held two other minor posts in government, he was almost unknown outside his home city. He had no important connections in Albany, the capital of New York State, and apparently he was not ambitious to hold even such a minor office as state Senator. Yet in 1881 Cleveland was catapulted into office as mayor of Buffalo. A year later he was nominated by the Democrats to run for governor of New York, and he won the election. Two years later he was nominated for President, and when he ran, in 1884, he was truly "the man nobody knows."

For many other reasons Cleveland should be well known to Americans, young and old, reasons that will be found in the story of his life and times, since as with most Presidents, the story of Cleveland tells much about the times in which he lived, and his character was shaped by the times and the people who surrounded him from his birth until he died.

Cleveland was born to the name Stephen Grover Cleveland, and his family called him Stephen during the first years of his life. He did not like the name, however, and when he was old enough to do so, he changed it by simply dropping the first name altogether, and used his middle name all during his adult life.

Cleveland is an old family name in America and it was well known by the time young Grover was born. One distant relation had been the founder of Cleveland, Ohio, a rough western town in the middle days of the nineteenth century. (A Moses Cleveland had come to the colonies as early as 1635.) But while the Clevelands were an old and honorable family in the new world, they did not prosper financially—at least Grover's branch of the family did not. They were artisans, small shopkeepers, and ministers.

A number of them were well-educated, including Grover's father, Richard Folley Cleveland, who went to school at Yale College and then to a religious seminary in

Baltimore to study for the Presbyterian ministry. In Baltimore, Richard met Ann Neal, a girl whose family was
wealthy enough to keep several servants, including slaves
—for this was long before the Civil War. Before he left
Baltimore, Richard Cleveland and Ann Neal were engaged, and after a year as pastor of a church in Connecticut, Richard returned to Baltimore and they were married.

It was hard for a girl who had grown up in the gentility
of southern society to accustom herself to the harshness
of a small Connecticut town. The people were proud of
their Yankee stock in this little town of Windham. Not
only were they Yankees, with the clipped non-committal
speech of the region, but the citizens of Windham were
narrow-minded, a characteristic they inherited directly
from their Puritan ancestors. Richard and Ann Cleveland
arrived in Windham in the fall of 1829. She was thought-
less enough to bring a Negro maid north with her, into a
town that was a center for the Abolitionists who were determined to stamp out slavery no matter what might happen.

Ann Cleveland was told in plain language that she would
have to send her Negro maid back home to Baltimore, for
it was not fitting for the wife of the minister to keep a
colored servant, and it did not matter that the maid had
begged Ann to bring her with her to the new home. The
maid had to go—and she did.

Neither could Ann Cleveland wear the gay, colored
dresses with their big hoop skirts which had been so popular
in her native South.

The ladies of the church told her that it was much more
fitting for the wife of the minister to be dressed in sober
blacks and grays.

The Clevelands bore life in Windham for three years, a
time in which two children were born to them. Finally,

they received an offer of a better post in Portsmouth, Virginia, and Richard decided to move there. The salary was very low—but at least he would really be the pastor of the church. He had been minister in Windham, but had never been given the title of pastor. Instead, he had been kept on a kind of probation for three years, so it was not painful for the Clevelands to leave Connecticut for the south. Two years later, however, Richard was offered a post in Caldwell, New Jersey, a suburb of New York City. Richard replaced Stephen Grover, who had been pastor of the Caldwell Presbyterian church since 1787.

On March 18, 1837, the fifth child was born to the Clevelands, and since Richard's friend, the old minister, had died just the previous year, they named the little boy Stephen Grover Cleveland to honor the old man. More children came along, almost one every year, until there were nine children in all in the Cleveland family. As the minister, Richard Cleveland received many gifts. His parishioners gave him free firewood, and he had the use of a gabled, two and a half story frame house, the best house in the entire village, but his salary was only $600, and even in the 1840's that did not go far towards supporting such a large family. Luckily, Ann Cleveland received a small income from her family's property to help support them.

Caldwell was Grover Cleveland's birthplace, but it was not the home town he remembered, for in 1841 Richard Cleveland accepted a post as minister in Fayetteville, a village on the Erie Canal in upstate New York, and it was here that Grover grew into his teens. Around 1850, when Henry Clay and Daniel Webster were struggling to save the Union, Grover Cleveland was fishing and playing pranks, roaming the hills around Fayetteville, and joining with other boys to remove the gates from villagers' fences on Hallowe'en. In the winter he went skating and sledding on the hills, and he was not above such pranks as attaching a long rope to the big bell in the tower of a local school house and ringing it late at night, when most villagers were asleep, to bring the men running from their beds half dressed to learn what disaster had brought about such a racket.

As the son of the minister, Grover had to work very hard. He took jobs running errands and raking leaves, and at one time during the harvest season he ran a corn-cutting machine for a local farmer, but he ran it so carelessly that he sliced the end off the middle finger of his left hand.

At home, the friendly, chubby boy lived under the strict discipline of a minister's family. He had to memorize his catechism, and came to know the Bible almost by heart. He attended all the church services on Sundays and other days—every Sunday there were two church services, Sunday school and an evening prayer meeting. Sunday—the Sabbath—began in the New England fashion at sundown on Saturday and lasted until sundown on Sunday. This meant no one in the God-fearing community did any more work than necessary during that period. All food was cooked before sundown, and the family ate cold meals on Saturday nights and Sundays. Only necessary work, such as feeding livestock or stoking fires, was undertaken on the Lord's day by the people of the town. In the minister's family absolutely no work was done if it could be avoided. Instead, the whole day Sunday was set aside for reflection—which Richard Cleveland hoped would be religious reflection—and for church affairs. None but religious books could be read that day. The only entertainment

Grover might enjoy on Sundays was a long walk in the orchard or in the formal garden his mother had made near the house.

Even though the Clevelands had very little money by modern standards still they were able to hire men to do heavy work around the house, and they kept a servant, a Canadian woman who did most of the cooking and served the meals for the family. In those days, however, all educated persons managed somehow to have servants, for without electricity or appliances it would have been extremely difficult for a housewife and mother to do anything but care for her house, if she had to do all the woman's chores alone.

In this atmosphere Grover Cleveland's character was shaped. He grew strong and big, because he was well fed and well tended by his mother; he grew up with good manners, because he was the son of a minister and was of gentle birth, related to the cultured and wealthy Dodge family of New York. He grew up full of pranks and a streak of wildness, as have many sons of ministers, repressed as they are in the austere atmosphere of high morality of a minister's home. He grew up with a distaste for church-going, which made itself apparent in his later life. Grover was not irreligious. He could and did quote copiously from the Bible in his adult years, but he showed very little interest in attending formal church services.

In Fayetteville, Grover went to school in a little red schoolhouse, one of the kind so well known in the early days of America; a single room in which pupils of all ages studied under a single schoolmaster, who did not hesitate to use a birch rod on the children if they misbehaved. When Grover was eleven years old, however, his family afforded a better education for him. He began to go to school in the local private academy, (whose bell he had rung at night) to have the benefit of a more classical education than that available at the district school. Even with limited money, the Rev. Richard Cleveland hoped to send his sons to college. Girls, of course, were not expected to be educated formally in those days. They spent most of their time at home learning the gentle arts from their mother: to sew and knit and crochet, to run a household, and perhaps to sing, or play a musical instrument, or to paint. But boys needed either a professional education to get ahead in the world, or some strong business connection to help them in the world of commerce. William Cleveland, the oldest son of the family, went away to Clinton, New York, to study at Hamilton College. Richard, the second son, decided to become an engineer—a profession he could learn by apprenticing himself to an uncle who was an engineer in Ohio. Grover was planning to go to college, too.

When Grover was 13 years old, his father was appointed to a better position with the American Home Missionary Society, and the family moved to Clinton, New York, where his brother William went to college. The girls in the family, then, could attend a female seminary, or finishing school, and the boys could look forward to completing a formal course of education. Grover attended the Clinton Academy that first year, studying Greek and Latin, which he would need to carry on his college work. But in the spring of 1852, when he was fifteen years old, Grover was forced to leave school and go to work to help earn his own way. He was offered a job clerking by Mr. McVicar, the keeper of the general store in Fayetteville, and he returned to work in that town at a salary of fifty dollars for the year.

In Fayetteville, as a clerk, Grover lived above the store. He arose before six o'clock in the morning, washed his face in a shallow basin or in the horse trough in the village square, and hurried back to the store. Before his employer appeared at seven in the morning, Grover had to open the store, light the fire, sweep the floor, be sure that all the goods were in place, and see that they were ready for business. Then, when the business day began, Grover made deliveries, ran other errands, pushed and pulled barrels and boxes of goods across the floor, and waited on customers when the storekeeper was busy. He and another boy used a single bare room in which there was a rope bed covered by a straw mattress, a night stand with a wash basin, but no pictures, rugs, or even a stove to keep them warm in winter. Their only heat came from a pipe which brought some warm air up from the store below.

It was hard work, but boys in those days expected hard work, and during the second year, when Grover had proved himself to the storekeeper, he was paid $100— twice as much as the year before. But after two years of clerking in the store, Grover decided to try again to go on to college, and returned to Clinton, hoping to enter Hamilton College. He had not been a brilliant student in preparatory school but he had shown interest in furthering his education, and in Fayetteville even when he was clerking he had helped organize a debating society.

At this same time, Grover's father was preparing to move the family to the little village of Holland Patent, not far from Utica, New York, on the Black River Railroad. The Rev. Richard Cleveland's health had suffered from the strenuous life of the professional missionary. He was forced to travel almost constantly, winter and summer, by coach, by steamer, by primitive railroad train, in days when travelling was uncomfortable, and when one might easily catch pneumonia in a drafty railroad car, or be blown up with the exploding boiler of one of the treacherous steamboats which plied the Hudson and other rivers.

Shortly after Grover's return to the family from Fayetteville, just three Sundays after the Rev. Cleveland had begun to preach in the pulpit of the Holland Patent church, the minister died, so suddenly that Grover was away from home in Utica with one of his sisters.

The death of his father put an end to Grover's hopes for a college education. There was no money for special education, there was scarcely enough money in the family to support the widow and the children who were not old enough to work for a living. Grover, a large boy, even if he was only sixteen years old, decided to go to work to help support his mother and the four young children. The family was far too proud to take charity, although a number of ministers offered to help educate the young ones. Mrs. Cleveland did accept an offer from the Holland Patent church members to let them keep the parsonage rent-free.

Grover first joined his brother William, the young man who had been educated at Hamilton College, when William went to work in New York City. William had been appointed a teacher in the New York Institution for the Blind. He found a place as an assistant for Grover, and from the fall of 1853 until the autumn of 1854 Grover lived and worked in the city. It was a dreary life, however, and Grover spent it mostly within the gray Gothic walls of the three-story institution working from nine in the morning until four-thirty in the afternoon, and only occasionally escaping the dreariness on a visit to the Dodges, his wealthy relatives, to attend a tea or musical performance, or to go sleighing in Central Park. Grover taught reading, writing, arithmetic, and geography to the younger children, but how well he taught or how he liked it remain largely mysteries, for in later years Cleveland had very little to say about his association with the school for the blind.

The following year, when he was seventeen, Grover returned to his mother's home in Holland Patent to study a little with a local teacher—mostly the Latin language. He also looked for work in Utica and in other towns and cities around the area, but found nothing that interested him or promised enough for the future to persuade him to remain there. He decided to make his way to Ohio, where he might find work and where he could count on the assistance of at least one relative—his uncle, the engineer. With another boy from Holland Patent and twenty-five dollars he borrowed from a friend of the family, Grover set out for the town of Cleveland, by way of Buffalo, intending to catch a boat and work his way along Lake Erie to the Ohio city, which still seemed to be the far west to Grover.

On their way west, the boys stopped off in Buffalo for a few days. Grover walked out to the Black Rock district, a suburb of Buffalo on the Niagara River, to visit another uncle, Lewis F. Allen, with whom he had spent a vacation five years earlier. His uncle asked Grover why he wanted to go west and learned that the boy really had no plans, except to make his fortune. Allen persuaded Grover to stay on in Black Rock by offering him free board and room and a job correcting the manuscript for a book. Allen was an expert stockbreeder who specialized in Shorthorn cattle, and each year he issued a revised herdbook for the guidance of other ambitious breeders. The checking of pedigrees was hard and painstaking work, and he needed assistance in it.

Grover agreed to stay on. He walked the two miles back into Buffalo and told his travelling companion that he would stay with his uncle, and then walked back to Black Rock. Grover did not know it then, but he would not leave the Buffalo area again, except for minor trips, until he had become an important man in the political affairs of the United States.

✪ the young lawyer

WHEN GROVER CLEVELAND came to Buffalo in 1855 he found a city that was exciting to live in and important to the growth of the American nation. A number of railroads served the city. The most important of them was the New York Central Railroad, then a tiny rail line which ran from the lake city to Albany, the capital of the state; it was small but important, because Buffalo was the key city of the Great Lakes region. From Buffalo goods could be shipped across to the west by water. From Buffalo the goods of the west were shipped south and east by train and by the Erie canal to New York City, which had already passed all the other ports to become the commercial hub of the nation.

Buffalo was a city of more than fifty thousand people when Grover Cleveland arrived there, and his uncle, Lewis Allen, was one of the most prominent citizens of the area. Black Rock, the suburb in which Lewis Allen lived, had been absorbed by the city of Buffalo the year before, but it was still regarded as "out of town." Allen's two-story fieldstone house overlooked busy Niagara Street, on which the horse cars travelled. From the back it also overlooked the Niagara River, where on Grand Island, in the middle of the stream, Allen had purchased a six hundred acre ranch for the raising of his Shorthorn and Devon cattle.

Grover went to work on the *American Herd Book* his uncle was preparing, lived in his uncle's house, and wandered in the orchard where apple, pear, and plum trees grew. Had Grover Cleveland wished to turn his hand to farming or to business, he would have found a sympathetic relative in his uncle. As it was, however, Grover had no regard for money-making or for work on the land. He had decided to follow the law, and while it would have been helpful had he been able to afford a college education, most of the lawyers, particularly in the west, had not studied at colleges but had learned law in the offices of practicing attorneys. When Grover had completed his work on the herd book and was ready to take his next step, Allen sent Grover to see Daniel Hibbard, a Black Rock neighbor and a justice of the peace. Grover's uncle and aunt preferred to see him stay in their suburban area rather than move to the center of the port city, a rough area which was full of saloons and German beerhalls. Each day there were so many fights on the waterfront that even in the daytime policemen always walked the dock area in pairs. Every night at least one or two sailors or travellers were found robbed and beaten, or murdered.

Grover had intended to ask Justice Hibbard to find a place for him to study the law in his office but when Hibbard asked some prying questions which Grover did not want to answer, the young man turned on his heel and marched out of the office. His uncle approved of this action and sent him to see Henry W. Rogers, head of the prominent Buffalo law firm of Rogers, Bowen, and Rogers. All three of the men in the firm had come up in the law the hard way, studying in the offices of other lawyers until they had sufficient knowledge to apply to the state supreme court for admission to the bar. Old Henry Rogers was not enthusiastic about taking a new clerk into the office, but Allen persisted on behalf of his nephew, and finally won Grover the right to study there. When Grover went to the office to begin his studies, Rogers pointed to a narrow knee-hole table covered with dust, equipped only with a shallow drawer at either end. He told the youngster to sit down, handed him a copy of Blackstone's *Commentaries,* and invited him to begin the study of the law. That book, the most widely-read in English common law, was the foundation of all the law western lawyers knew. It had served this firm well, for this was the original firm of Millard Fillmore, a Whig lawyer and politician, and then the most important citizen of Buffalo. He had been the President of the United States, succeeding to office from the vice-presidency on the death of President Zachary Taylor in 1850.

All the members of the firm of Rogers, Bowen, and Rogers were Whigs until the year 1856, when the Whig party broke up and the Republican party was formed. But that year, Denis Bowen, one of the partners, joined the Democratic party, and while Grover Cleveland's uncle was a Whig (who became a Republican), Grover leaned in favor of the Democrats and marched in their torchlight parades. Cleveland was only nineteen years old in 1856, but he was as staunch a supporter of Democratic Presidential candidate James Buchanan as any in the nation and rejoiced that fall when Buchanan was elected.

Three years later, when Cleveland was twenty two years old, he was admitted to the New York State bar, although he remained with the firm as chief clerk at a salary of $600 a year. As a junior attorney he was earning as much money each year as his father had earned during most of his lifetime.

As he labored in the law offices, Grover continued to spend much time on the Allen farm at Black Rock. He went there, he said, to help with the crops or to work on the cattle brand book for which his uncle continued to

WINGATE COLLEGE LIBRARY
WINGATE, N. C.

pay him fifty or sixty dollars a year, but much pleasurable fishing was done as well.

When he had begun clerking in the law office, Grover had moved into the middle of Buffalo since it was too long a journey from the Allen home at Black Rock to the office, and Grover spent many hours each day in the law office. One day Grover stayed so long at his corner desk, with his head glued to his books, that when he arose he found all the others had gone and that he was locked in for the night. He had begun, even in these early days, to display the perseverance and aptitude for long hours of work that were to characterize his adult life. Also, he had begun to show his independence and a streak of wildness. He spent much time in beerhalls and restaurants drinking beer, of which he was very fond, and singing, sometimes until the small hours of the morning. His aunt, Mrs. Allen, was not pleased with the companions Grover found in the saloons and told him so. He did not change, but the social differences between them, and the differences in political leanings, began to show, and it was not long before it was apparent that Grover Cleveland was growing away from his relatives.

There were two distinct sides to Grover's character. First was the hard-working, stubborn young man, who glorified in difficult tasks and took pains always to do his best. Long hours of work meant nothing to him. He was perfectly capable of staying up the whole night working on a legal brief—looking up points of law that would help his arguments. Then, in the morning, after a wash and several cups of hot coffee, he was ready to undertake another day, without sleep. He was also capable of staying up most of the night with his gay companions, even staying up so late he was scarcely good for work at all on the following day. He liked high life, and he loved to drink great quantities of beer. Consequently, even as a young man, the chubby Cleveland grew fat, with a heavy bull neck, a slightly drooping mustache, and a growing paunch which hung over his beltline.

He continued to work hard and save his money, even as he enjoyed himself in the evenings after working hours. Every month he sent money home to his mother in Holland Patent, and each year the amount was more than the year before. It was not long before Grover was earning $1000 a year as chief clerk for the law firm—and this when he was less than twenty-five years old.

From 1858, when he had turned twenty-five, Grover took an active part in local Democratic party politics. He was a loyal Democrat now, but he was also a loyal Union man. So while he supported the Democratic candidacy of Stephen A. Douglas for the Presidency in 1860, he agreed with Dean Richmond, the river boat and railroad tycoon, who completely denied the right of any state to secede from the Union. Not all the Clevelands felt so strongly, for like many other families just before the Civil War, the Clevelands were divided in their opinion about slavery. Grover's elder brother William had married a southern girl, and William had little sympathy for the Union cause, but Grover was one of those Democrats called "War Democrats" who supported the Union wholeheartedly.

It may seem strange that when the war actually came, Grover Cleveland did not enlist in the Union army to fight for the cause in which he believed. His brother Lewis Frederick enlisted in the Thirty-second New York volunteers in 1861 and rose to become a lieutenant. His brother Richard Cecil joined an Indiana regiment in 1861 and remained in the Union army until 1864. Grover did not join the army at all. In 1862 he had worked hard for the election of the state and local Democratic candidates, and he was appointed Assistant District Attorney in Erie county. Actually, the District Attorney was sick during much of his term of office, and Grover did the bulk of the work. He had not been in office six months, however, when the Union began to draft men for army service. It was the summer of 1863. The draftees were selected from among the names of all the able-bodied men in the community, whose names were put in a drum-shaped box which turned on an axle. Officials then drew names out of the box. If the man who was called did not want to go into service, he could buy an exemption by paying $300 to a substitute who would go in his place.

On the first day of the call, Grover Cleveland's name was drawn. He held an important post in the local government, and he had assumed much of the responsibility for taking care of his mother. His younger brother Fred offered to go in Grover's place, but Fred had already been in the service and had fought once. Grover borrowed $300 and hired a substitute instead.

When the war ended, Cleveland, as chief assistant in the District Attorney's office, was chosen by the Democratic party to run for District Attorney. At that time, he was rooming with Lyman K. Bass, another young attorney, and oddly enough, Bass was chosen to run for the same office on the Republican ticket. The pair met every evening to drink beer and debate, in good humor. When the election came, Cleveland had carried most of the wards in Buffalo itself, but Bass was elected District Attorney by the votes of Republican farmers and small townsmen of the outlying area. That was the end of Grover Cleveland's political career for a number of years.

Grover settled down in Buffalo to practice law. He had held one minor elective office during the war years, the job of ward supervisor, but he was not to run for office again until 1870. Instead, he began to establish himself as a lawyer, and he practiced with several partners, including a man who was to become a dear friend, Oscar Folsom. It was not many years before this law firm was well known in Buffalo and throughout the western part of the state.

Cleveland did a great amount of work for the New York Central Railroad. When Commodore Vanderbilt took over the New York Central and combined it with two other railroads to bring it from Buffalo to New York City by way of Albany and the Hudson River, he brought Chauncey Depew into the Central organization. Depew offered Cleveland the job as counsel for the railroad at the western end of the line, but Cleveland did not want to spend all his time working for one client, and refused.

Cleveland was invited to be chairman of the Erie County Democratic organization but refused that job as well, since he was trying to make his fortune and the political job would have taken most of his time. But the offer indicates how well-respected he was in his party, and newspaper praise of the young lawyer as an up-and-coming member of the bar indicated how well liked he was by the leaders of Buffalo.

The population of Buffalo now had more than doubled; in the 1860's it was around 100,000, which meant more industry, more people in business, and more legal business. Cleveland avoided criminal law when he could. He preferred business dealings and civil suits. He was a good lawyer, a careful one, and also a very soft-hearted man. One time, a woman came to him to ask for help after she had defaulted on her mortgage and was about to be evicted from her home. Legally, the case was clearly against her, but Cleveland won it for the lady, in a way. He paid off the mortgage himself, so she and her children would not

be evicted, and later he chuckled when he remembered
that she had the best case of all—a family to bring up.

Cleveland had lived in a number of boarding houses, a
carefree bachelor, taking his meals and his pleasures where
he found them. He liked nothing better than to stop in
at one of a half dozen restaurants in Buffalo for a stein of
beer and a German meal. At least once he was involved in
a street brawl (over a political matter) with an Irish Democrat named Mike Falvey. The two fought for a half hour
up and down the street until they were exhausted, then
adjourned to a nearby saloon, a place called Gillick's, and
drank each other's health.

In 1868 Cleveland was a delegate to the state Democratic convention, but he was not a particularly outspoken
delegate, and most historians make no mention of his at-
tendance. He was an important lawyer in Buffalo by this
time. He had moved his offices into the Weed block, a
square white five-story building, and he moved his apartment into the back of the building, despite the fact that
it was an office building and not a residential building.
He ate his meals in a saloon or in a French restaurant
down the street and spent his evenings in bars, serenading
with other young men of this gaslight period in which the
famous "barbershop quartets" really did exist.

In 1870, Cleveland again decided to run for public office
—this time for sheriff. Usually men of education, lawyers
in particular, would not run for such a post, but Cleveland
was an odd kind of lawyer: he had as many friends among
the rough sailors and saloon keepers of the waterfront as
he had among the quiet businessmen of the better parts of
the city, and he did not care at all for the company of the
ladies of proper society.

There was talk at this time about running Cleveland
for Congress, but when the local Democratic convention

was held, the leaders decided to put his name up for sheriff. Cleveland was well pleased, for the sheriff received fees for performing various legal duties, and he could expect, quite honestly, to receive an income of forty or fifty thousand dollars during his term of office. He ran and was elected by a narrow margin of three hundred and three votes. At the age of thirty-three, Cleveland now expected to earn more money in public office than he could make as a lawyer.

As sheriff, Grover spent much of his time fishing and hunting. He was not a law enforcement officer by nature, any more than he was a great student or a man interested in the land. He did love the outdoors, but in town he was happiest when sitting in a hotel lounge with a group of other men, talking, telling jokes, and drinking beer. His interest in fishing led him to become one of the founders of the Beaver Island club. A group of young men joined together and bought an island in the Niagara River. They put up a clubhouse and used the island in the spring to shoot ducks and in the summer for fishing, boating and swimming.

But as sheriff of Erie County, Grover Cleveland did give the first indication of the kind of public official he would become in later years. He hired a lawyer named W. L. G. Smith to become undersheriff and gave Smith authority to handle the administration of details. Matters of policy were kept in Cleveland's own sphere, and it was in matters of public policy that he made his reputation. Cleveland's opponent in the election, Colonel John B. Weber, later said that Cleveland looked down on ward politicians and refused them the illegal favors they had so long enjoyed as part of the process of government.

To understand the reasons for this, it must be remembered that at the end of the Civil War, the Democratic

party had been discredited in most parts of the Union. A
great number of Democrats had opposed the war because,
before 1860, the major strength of the Democrats was in
the south. After 1861, it was natural enough for the northern Democrats to yearn for the days when they had the
strongest party and to work for an end to the war, under
any conditions. Most northern Democrats had no use for
slavery, but they did not feel that slavery was an issue that
should have been raised at all. They agreed with one old
southern leader, who before the Civil War had told an
outraged northerner that the American government policy
favored slavery—in other words, that the federal government was committed to slavery. These northern Democrats came to be known as "Copperheads," and the word—
the name of a poisonous snake—became a curse in the language of the 1860's and 1870's. Cleveland, of course, was
not a Copperhead, but an out-and-out War Democrat who
believed in the suppression of the Confederacy, and yet,
so strong were emotions at the end of the Civil War, that
almost all Democrats were suspected of disloyalty to the
Union.

   In a sense, then, outside New York City and a few other
strongholds of the Democratic party, the nation was ruled
by a single political organization—the Republican party.
The Republicans held too much power for too long a period, and each year they became just a little bit less rigid
in their standards of honesty. Nor were standards of government nearly so high in the middle of the nineteenth
century as they became in the twentieth century. It was
quite acceptable for a public official to hire his friends in
important jobs, once he was elected. The idea of civil
service—the merit system of appointment and of holding
jobs—was quite new, and most politicians sneered at the
new-fangled ways.

In cities and towns like Buffalo, the aldermen and the mayor ran the city to suit themselves. The voters, both Republicans and Democrats, voted to please their ward bosses. When they did please them, and the bosses were in power, the voters could go to the ward organization for jobs on the streets, or for appointments to the police department, or to get a city contract—without worrying about competitive bidding.

Thus, city jobs helped the political party that was in power and let the politicians make their fortunes. The party out of power always claimed that the others were crooks—and everybody expected them to make that claim, for the fact was that in those days both parties indulged in practices we would call "crooked" today.

After Cleveland was elected sheriff, he came to the attention of the Democratic party quickly and unfavorably. The three previous sheriffs of Erie County had all been Democrats, and they had rewarded other Democrats with rich government contracts. Cleveland discovered that the county was being cheated by the tradesmen under these contracts. When the contractor who supplied firewood for the jail made his delivery, Cleveland checked the delivery and found it was short in weight; he discovered that supplies of flour and oatmeal were not being delivered as stated in the bills, and that there were other irregularities in the deliveries. So Cleveland broke the contracts with these suppliers and announced that in the future all contracts would be made after public bids were taken. Then the man who offered the best contract to the government would get the job.

The Democratic party of Buffalo was annoyed. Cleveland, they had discovered, was not an ordinary politician.

In this office, Cleveland also began to display the strength of character for which he became famous in later years.

Under the law, the sheriff was responsible for carrying out executions of men who had been convicted of murder and sentenced to be hanged. At this time executions were carried out locally, and not in state penitentiaries. In the past, the sheriff of the county had given one of his deputies the unpleasant job of pulling the lever which would drop the convicted man off the scaffold and out of the living world, but Cleveland refused to deputize one of his men for the job, on the firm principle that he had been elected by the people and that the unpleasant task was his alone. He personally executed two men during his term of office, much as he hated to do so.

At the end of that one term, Cleveland had no desire to run for re-election, and the Democratic party would have balked at any rate, so difficult had he been in matters of party patronage which they held dear. Cleveland formed a new law firm with Lyman K. Bass, the roommate who had defeated him in the race for District Attorney, and settled down to what appeared to be a long and increasingly successful career as a lawyer in Buffalo. He had no further thoughts of public office; he had saved $20,000 during his term as sheriff and had no further worries about money.

As the years passed, Cleveland grew in stature and in bulk. He was not a heavy eater, and he drank little distilled liquor, but he drank beer constantly. It was not long before he weighed two hundred pounds, and then two hundred and twenty-five pounds, and then more. His friends began to call him Jumbo, in addition to "Big Cleve" and "Big Steve" and "Grove." He was a man of many nicknames, because he was so well-liked by bachelor and club friends in Buffalo. Yet after he became sheriff, and completed his term, Cleveland became more dignified. He usually appeared in public in a black broadcloth suit, with clean white linen shirt and necktie, and a top hat. Sometimes he even went fishing in this costume, his friends claimed. He continued to play pinochle and a card game called "Sixty-six" in Louis Goetz's restaurant, or Bass's saloon, or Schenkelberger's restaurant, where he enjoyed the sausages and sauerkraut. But he also helped found the dignified City Club and spent a great deal of his time there.

Many of Cleveland's friends wondered why he did not marry now that he had become financially independent and his law practice was flourishing. For several reasons Cleveland was to remain a bachelor for a long time to come. First, he liked the society of men, and he detested dancing and the formalities of the mixed society of upper middle class Buffalo. He loved fishing as much as he hated dancing, and he was less fearful of a charging moose than of a society matron bearing down on him, daughter in hand. There were also two other reasons for his bachelorhood, one of them concealed until he ran for President, and the other unsuspected until he had attained the highest office in the nation.

Sometime in 1873 Cleveland had been introduced to a young widow named Maria Crofts Halpin, who had come to Buffalo from Pennsylvania, where she left two children. Mrs. Halpin was well educated; she spoke French fluently; she was tall, slender, and attractive; and she liked the society of men. Grover became involved with Mrs. Halpin romantically, as did a number of other men in Buffalo. In 1874, a son was born to her, and she said that Cleveland was the father. Cleveland was not sure this was true, but the other men involved were all married and he was not, so he accepted the responsibility for the child, although he did not want to marry the mother. Mrs. Halpin, after Cleveland refused to marry her, took to drinking heavily and neglecting the baby. Cleveland heard of this and asked a friend, Roswell Burroughs, to handle the matter, since he did not want to become involved further. Temporarily, Mrs. Halpin was committed to an insane asylum; the child was put in an orphan asylum; and after a few weeks, Mrs. Halpin went to Niagara Falls with money Cleveland had given her to establish a business there, since she had learned the department store trade while working in Buffalo.

In Niagara Falls, Mrs. Halpin became lonesome for her child and returned to Buffalo and kidnaped him from the orphan asylum. The boy was returned, however, and later was adopted by a family in western New York, disappearing from Cleveland's life and from Mrs. Halpin's life, too. The case was not widely publicized, even in Buffalo, and for the moment, no more attention was paid to it, either by Cleveland or by anyone around him.

The third reason for Cleveland's continued refusal to marry was the assumption of some family responsibilities of his own. Oscar Folsom, his old friend and former law partner, was killed one day while driving in his buggy. As with many lawyers before and since, Folsom had left no will, but a wife and daughter who had to be looked after, and Cleveland was appointed administrator of the Folsom estate. Thereafter, the Folsoms became as close to Cleveland as though they had been related to him. He had trouble enough, and family responsibility enough, without a marriage for which he felt he was ill-suited.

He plodded along in Buffalo, showing no great drive or brilliance in the law, but a great amount of strength and firmness when his interest was aroused. He continued to be an active member of the Democratic party, but never spoke of seeking office. He spent his days in legal affairs or fishing or hunting with his cronies, and his nights in hotel lobbies, in the living room of his comfortable apartment in the Weed block, or in a club or restaurant playing cards and drinking with his friends. Except for the bar association and the City Club he seemed to have few civic interests. Altogether he was the type of man who seemed to have great solidity, but no imagination or drive. His friends thought of him as something like the rock of Gibraltar, solid and stern as granite; a man to be leaned on, but not one whose ways could be changed. Certainly, in the spring of 1881, when his law practice was the only matter on his mind except duck hunting, no one suspected that in less than four years Grover Cleveland, lawyer, would be the most famous man in all America.

✧ the mayor,
a reformer

CLEVELAND'S PATH to fame seems almost unexplainable to anyone who does not understand the state of mind of Americans in the last years of the 1870's and the beginnings of the 1880's. After the Civil War the level of morality in American cities fell sharply. Men who had seen the horror of war had been corrupted. In their absence lesser men had taken over government.

The two federal administrations of Ulysses S. Grant were the most corrupt and least defensible of any in the history of the nation. Cabinet officers, from the Secretary of War on down, and persons close to Grant were involved in theft from the federal treasury. In Congress, men gave away public lands and rights in exchange for personal fortunes. It was an age of looseness and expansion in every way; the railroads were sweeping west, industries were growing up all across the country; fortunes were being made in land and livestock, and in every possible exploitation of natural resources or of men and women. A man might make a fortune overnight, in a gold mine or a street railroad franchise or in a Wall Street speculation. The speculators, like the others, cared little who suffered in the process.

In the seventies the city of Buffalo had fallen into the

hands of a group of corrupt politicians. In those days, such groups were called "rings," and famous among these circles were the Tweed Ring of New York City, the Whiskey Ring of St. Louis, and the Washington Ring, which controlled the street railroad franchise in the nation's capital and looted the public treasury. Buffalo's ring was composed of politicians of both the Republican and Democratic parties—so the Buffalo ring had managed to stay in control of the city government for ten years. The Republicans of Buffalo were most prominent in the ring, but Democratic aldermen were involved, too, and they kept their party from raising the issue of corruption as a campaign question, year after year.

In 1878, the ring elected a Democratic mayor, a German-born brewer named Solomon Scheu, who was not personally corrupt (he did not need money) but who never interfered with the thievery of the aldermen who ran the city. The next mayor was a Republican named Brush, but he had no more interest in good government than Mayor Scheu, and under the Brush administration taxes went up remarkably. It cost $60,000 more to run the fire department than before and $25,000 more to run the police department, but the citizens of Buffalo could see no improvement in law enforcement or fire prevention.

Generally speaking, the Buffalo ring was controlled by the Republicans, but John C. Sheehan, leader of the Democrats in the First Ward, and the most important Democrat in the city, was also a member of the ring. By 1880 the ring had become so powerful that its members were not too careful to conceal their thievery from the public, and a number of prominent citizens became angry. In 1881, a friend of Cleveland's, Peter Doyle, was elected County Chairman of the Democratic party. Doyle, an honest man himself, decided it was time to clean house

and throw out the crooked Republicans and the crooked
Democrats who had been running the town for so long.
He appointed a committee of five men to find a strong,
honest man to run for mayor in the fall of 1881.

That committee went forth one day in the fall of 1881
to find a suitable candidate among the businessmen of the
city. But after an afternoon of tramping along Commercial
Street, climbing the steep stairs to the business offices, and
being turned down time and again, the members had still
not found their candidate by evening. The businessmen
of the community were much too busy making money to
soil their hands with politics, particularly since it was well
known by this time that the political leaders in Buffalo
were very unscrupulous indeed.

The committee had called on every prominent Democrat in the city, on bankers, merchants, and the man who
as President of the Board of Trade had been crying for
years in behalf of "better government" until he was asked
to run for the office of mayor himself. Then he refused
and offered, instead, a few hundred dollars to add to the
campaign fund for better government.

The committee members were tired, disgusted, and in-
censed at the refusal of the Democratic businessmen to do
their duty. They stopped in at Dringer's saloon to have
a drink and a meal and discuss their next move. While
they sat around the table, arguing the merits of the various
possible candidates, Grover Cleveland walked into the
room and came to the table to join them.

On seeing Cleveland, the committee members immediately thought of him as a candidate for the office. He refused, saying he was a lawyer, not a businessman, and that
he did not want either that job or any public office.

But as the committee members continued to talk, they
realized that Cleveland, with his bulk, his drooping heavy

mustache, and his reputation in the community for solid
integrity, had exactly the attributes needed to reform the
city administration. Cleveland, in other words, was a
"heavyweight," whose very size somehow lent an air of dignity and responsibility to the politician.

Eventually, that evening, the committee persuaded
Cleveland to accept the call. He had only one condition:
the rest of the candidates for city office must be acceptable
to him. In that demand, Cleveland was making sure that
if he was elected as a reform mayor, the men who went
into office with him would not be able to destroy all his
efforts before he even began. Specifically, Cleveland insisted on getting rid of John Sheehan, who was the incumbent controller of the city, and as such was in charge of
the disbursement of city funds.

That demand called for a great deal of sacrifice by the
Democrats, for Sheehan stood high in the councils of the
party. But there was no other course, if the movement for
reform was to be successful. The Republicans were running a man who had been president of the Common Council, who was a prominent member of the Grand Army of
the Republic (the Civil War veterans organization) and
Grand Master of the Ancient Order of United Workmen
(a guild-like workingmen's organization in the days before
the power of labor unions). Once in power, that Republican would be almost impossible to oust in future elections.

Finally, it was arranged. Sheehan was frightened off by
the implied threat that Cleveland knew about his dishonest behaviour in office and that Cleveland would expose
him publicly after the election. A Cleveland man was put
in Sheehan's place on the ticket.

Grover Cleveland was actually nominated for mayor at
the Democratic city convention on October 25th, three
days after he had encountered the nominating committee,

quite by chance, in the midst of their hunt for a reform candidate.

Cleveland was a reformer, but he was also a reformer the working man could understand. He told the Democratic convention that he could see no reason why the affairs of the city should not be managed with the same care and economy as business. He said that public office was a position of trust, and that the people had a right to demand honesty in government. But when he campaigned and told the voters these same things, he did so, often as not, standing atop a beer table in a saloon, having first bought a drink for all the voters in sight.

Cleveland's major concern in this campaign was the waterfront area, for this was Sheehan's First Ward, and it was here that the Republicans and Democrats banded together to make the "deals" by which they stole from the city. Cleveland campaigned hardest in the waterfront area, amid the six hundred saloons of Buffalo. He spent the Saturday night before election visiting saloons. And here, in this last night of campaigning, he threw down the gauntlet, named his enemies, referred to their collusion, and called on the voters to support him for honest government. He earned, in those furious days of campaigning, the name of "a man of courage."

Cleveland attacked the Republican conduct of government and the strange system under which the county treasurer received the interest on public money which was in his charge. He promised city workers that they would be paid weekly instead of once a month. He was harassed by old soldiers who wanted him to contribute to various causes and he refused to contribute, saying he was tired of the "old soldier business." A few years before, when the Republicans so successfully reminded the voters of the awfulness of the Civil War, Cleveland would have courted defeat by refusing any demand by the soldiers. But times had changed, and the entire country was tired of being reminded, endlessly, of the Civil War. Buffalo was no exception. As if to prove that point, and the feeling for reform, Cleveland ran far ahead of his ticket. The Republican candidates for state offices carried Buffalo handily, but Cleveland won the mayoralty by a majority of nearly 3600 votes. He polled more than 15,000 to less than 12,000 for his opponent and pulled the candidates for lesser city offices in with him.

So on January 1, 1882, when he was forty-four years old, Grover Cleveland took the oath of office as mayor of Buffalo, and declared war on the dishonest ring which controlled the Common Council of his city. There were sixteen Republicans and ten Democrats on that council, most of them agents of the conspirators who intended to keep on stealing public funds, no matter who was mayor.

In his inaugural message, Cleveland came straight to the heart of the matter. He had not been elected to devise new policies for Buffalo, but to stop the theft of public money, and that was what he proposed to do. His first task would be to stop skulduggery in the street department; second, to put an end to favored treatment of certain friendly newspapers; and third, to clean up the corruption in school construction.

For several years the city of Buffalo had been paying twenty-six cents a foot to contractors who built sidewalks along city property, while private citizens could get the same work done for fifteen cents a foot. Even worse, Controller Sheehan and the other members of the ring had worked out a system under which no one checked the bills paid by the city. The city auditor was to check the bills, but the council had allowed him only to check the arithmetic. He was not allowed to examine the bills sent by contractors to see if the work had actually been done, and if the city was getting fair prices and good values.

This opening message from the new mayor was only the beginning of the war against corruption. Nor was Cleveland content only to wipe out corruption. In a short time he had adopted a plan to solve the nagging sewage problem in Buffalo, putting an end to epidemic diseases carried in the filth, and bringing clean water to the city.

In the last half of the nineteenth century many of the bursting cities of the east and middle west were discovering suddenly that they had "sewage problems." Most of these cities were located on some body of water, and in the beginning, when the first traders had built their shacks, the river or the lake had served well enough to supply drinking water and to carry off human wastes. All that was needed was the elemental understanding that one drank from water that flowed upstream from the city and threw the waste material into the water downstream. Gravity and the attractions of the sea were supposed to take care of the rest of the problem.

But as the land became more heavily populated, the waste materials from one city interfered with the drinking water of the city a few miles down-stream. The suburbs grew upstream and downstream from the city, and in a few years the sewage problem became serious.

In Buffalo, the problem had become acute by the time Cleveland was elected mayor. Buffalo was built on ground that sloped above Lake Erie, so it might seem that it was no serious problem to drain the sewage into the lake, far from the limits of the city. But early in Buffalo's history the Erie canal had been built into the city. The canal was a blessing. It had been as responsible for the growth of Buffalo as any other combination of factors. But in putting the canal through, the builders had run a section,

known as the Main and Hamburg Street Canal, across the
natural drainage line of the city. The filth of Buffalo
drained into the canal and sat there in the stagnant water,
rotting. The townsmen built a water wheel at the edge
of Lake Erie to create a current, but the current only
drove the refuse farther up the canal, endangering the
health of other areas as well.

When Mayor Grover Cleveland took office, he discovered that in 1880, 4,000 persons died in Buffalo—and that
a third of those who died were victims of epidemic diseases. Typhoid fever, a disease carried in sewage, was the
greatest killer of all.

Cleveland drew attention to the matter of sewage control. He offered a plan for the employment of the best
possible firm of engineers to supervise the building of a
new sewer system which would empty into the Niagara
River. To assure the most efficiency, he proposed a novel
departure in city management—he asked the city government to request that the state legislature appoint a special
sewer commission. Cleveland realized that in the three
years it would take to finish the sewer system, the terms
of all the elected officials of Buffalo would expire. If the
city was to have continuity of management, then a special
commission was the only way to secure it.

When they heard of his plan, the members of the Buffalo Common Council began to complain. It was an out-
rage, they said, to take the government out of the hands
of the politicians and put it in the hands of the people.
They did not state it that directly, of course, but that was
the tenor of their complaint. And in their upset, they were
joined by city officials whose professional interests were
being affected. The city engineer claimed he was quite
capable of doing the job without calling in outsiders.

The councilmen increased the size of the city engineer's

staff to accommodate the new work, in spite of Cleveland's objection. When a state senator introduced a bill in the legislature to create the commission Cleveland wanted, the council condemned the senator's interference. But in the end, Cleveland had his way because nearly all the Buffalo newspapers supported his stand, and in those days before radio and television, newspapers had a far more important place in American affairs than they do today. The newspapers were the only reliable public carriers of information. While the editors stoutly proclaimed their views and often colored their reporting of public affairs, the reading public knew how to read newspapers and get information from them. By twentieth-century standards there were quite a few newspapers in Buffalo, too, a half dozen important English language papers and at least three important publications in German.

Nearly all of these papers supported Cleveland in his argument with the council, and eventually the council backed down. The commission was created by the legislature.

The council continued to delay, however. First the councilmen voted long-term bonds to finance the sewer system. The long-term bonds were desirable for investors, but not for the city, for they meant a much larger interest expense. Cleveland vetoed the act. Then, a few weeks later, when Cleveland sent his list of sewer commission appointees to the council, the councilmen retaliated by rejecting all five names. Cleveland sent the same five names back again. On the second submission the names were accepted, the commission was established, and the work was begun. Earlier, under the old system of corruption, an advertisement for bids for the sewer job had brought in a low bid of more than $1,500,000 for construction of the system. The commission consulted with pro-

fessional sanitary engineers and finally adopted a plan
which eventually cost the people of Buffalo only half
that amount, yet did the job in the best way known at that
time.

In the sewage fight Cleveland established his place in
the history of the city of Buffalo, but it is doubtful if that
one struggle would have brought him to national prominence. Nor could it be isolated from the rest of Mayor
Cleveland's policies and actions. He began, on his very
first day in office, to wage war on corruption, and as the
citizens of the city of Buffalo discovered that it was possible
to be governed honestly, they cheered.

He vetoed one dishonest bill after another. The councilmen proposed to buy the favor of the German language
newspapers by paying them to print reports of the council
meetings. Cleveland vetoed the bill. The city had long
accepted gifts of land for streets and had then allowed private real estate developers the privilege of laying out the
streets any way they wanted. Consequently, Buffalo was
growing without plan, with wide streets, narrow streets,
crooked streets and useless streets. Cleveland put an end
to this zoning farce and forced the real estate men to build
their streets to city specifications.

He supported measures to clean up the filthy dairies in
the city, and other moves to fill in wells in the middle of
the city which were contaminated. By this time the city
of Buffalo had a planned water system, but some residents
within the city resented the idea of paying for water, which
they had always drawn from the ground near their houses.
A few refused to connect to the mains and continued to
use the wells. Cleveland fought the issue to a finish, and
succeeded in closing the wells. He said this:

"There is no place in this enlightened age for the prop-
osition that the authorities of a city may maintain an un-

wholesome public well, known to be such, even though the people are willing to take the risk to life and health in the use of the water."

These were radical views for the time, for they made it quite clear that Cleveland had adopted a new view of government. In the beginnings of the American nation, government had been a responsibility assumed for the most part by the wealthy and cultured men of the towns, states, and the nation. The wealthy were the only citizens who could take time from labor to govern. Until the Civil War this was true, although in such large cities as New York professional politicians came into prominence ten years before the war. Fernando Wood, a mayor of New York City in the 1850's, was such a man. Previous mayors, who were gentlemen of an older era, found Wood and his city government beneath contempt.

Why? Because this new class of professional politicians was neither gentle, nor in most cases even educated. With the emergence of two strong national political parties on the American scene, it became common enough for a man to decide to adopt politics as a profession. Through holding government office the politician reaped his personal rewards. Since he was usually a poor man, the temptations to become rich were very great, and both political parties tended to wink at cheating in public office—as long as the party was able to control the officeholder enough to secure political jobs and contracts for loyal party members.

By 1882, the entire nation was sick of this corruption, and Mayor Cleveland, in Buffalo, was showing one way to put government into the hands of the people and to make sure that the citizens received the best government possible. He became known as the "veto mayor" and his vetoes of bills which would have literally robbed the public treasury were reported widely in the Buffalo press. It was

not long before some of these actions were reported elsewhere. He also achieved a certain amount of state recognition by travelling to Albany to make a plea for clemency
in the case of a Buffalo man convicted of murder. Under
normal conditions, this was scarcely the action expected
of a mayor, but Cleveland had studied the case and was
convinced, as was nearly all of Buffalo, that an injustice
had been done. Yet the convicted man, Martin Flanagan,
would be hanged unless the governor commuted the sentence. Cleveland pleaded so well in Albany that the sentence was commuted, and incidentally the whole odd affair
came to the attention of newspapers throughout the state.

Cleveland was fortunate in one regard. He had created
a personal fortune large enough that he was never tempted
in any way. Before he entered office he was one of two or
three of the most prominent attorneys in Buffalo. He had
told a friend several years before that he had $75,000, and he
continued to be a partner in the law firm which bore his
name during his tenure as mayor. He could not, certainly,
have existed on his mayor's salary of $2500 a year.

Since he had no personal financial worries, Cleveland
was able to spend all his energies on his chosen task of
securing good government for Buffalo. The most prominent single action of his administration was a veto of the
city's street cleaning contract.

In June, after Cleveland had been in office for six
months, the council awarded a contract for cleaning the
streets to a man named George Talbot, who had bid a
price of $422,500 to do the job for five years. The Talbot
bid was suspicious in every way. He had first put in a bid
for $372,500 and had then raised it. Among the other bid-
ders was one who said he would do the job for $313,500.
Yet Talbot had been selected by the council to do the job.
There was every indication that $50,000 or $100,000 of the

money would find its way into the pockets of some of the
councilmen. Cleveland vetoed the council action, called it
an attempt to betray the people, and created such a stir
that the contract was awarded to the lowest bidder. Cleveland's actions appealed to the press, which gave great publicity to his reform movement. His bulk and his heavy,
severe face showed the honesty of a Sunday school teacher
and the strength of a professional boxer. He was heavy
handed and blunt, which appealed to the press. His statements about public office were severe and uncompromising. One of his thoughts was later rephrased and circu-
lated across the nation: "A public office is a public trust."

Not only Buffalo, but all New York State was tired of
corruption. Buffalo had its ring, but New York State had
not yet recovered from the thievery of a succession of dishonest legislatures; the thefts of Boss Tweed, who was for
a time a state senator; and the dishonesties under the administration of Governor John T. Hoffman, a man who is
remembered only because he was the creature of Tweed
and Tammany Hall.

The time was ripe, in the summer of 1882, for a man
like Grover Cleveland to move rapidly in the political
world.

✮ the honest man in albany

IN THE SPRING of 1882 the Democratic party of the state of New York was badly divided in its loyalties. Two outstanding candidates sought nomination as governor: a wealthy young man named Roswell P. Flower, who had earned some reputation as a ward politician and financier first in upstate Watertown, and then in New York City; and General Henry Slocum of Brooklyn, another of the Civil War commanders, who was known principally for his association with General William Tecumseh Sherman on the famous march through Georgia.

The party was split into three groups. First, there was the Tilden organization, which included almost all Democrats outside of New York City. This organization was the remainder of the personal following of Samuel J. Tilden, who had run unsuccessfully for President in the fraudulent election of 1876. The Tilden organization backed General Slocum, apparently for no other reason than because the Tilden leaders disliked Roswell Flower.

The second important party organization was Tammany Hall, the Democratic organization of New York City. Tammany leaders could not agree on a candidate. The most important point to them was to be sure to back a winner.

The third Democratic organization was called the County Democracy. This was a reform group, centered on Manhattan Island in New York City, which had been formed largely to counter Tammany Hall's influence among Democrats.

The County Democracy refused to join the Tilden group in backing Slocum, although Brooklyn Democrats, of course, joined behind their townsman.

It would be heroic to say that Grover Cleveland captured the imagination of New York Democrats so sweepingly that he was rushed into prominence in the state Democratic party without his knowledge or apparent wishes, but such a statement would not be truthful. After only six months in the office of mayor, Cleveland was awake to his own potential power in the political affairs of his state, and his ambition was aflame. It is truthful to say that Cleveland rose to prominence because he was a diligent reformer, but that is not reason enough, for there have been other diligent reformers, before and since, and yet no such man ever rose faster than Cleveland.

One of the leaders of the independent upstate Democrats was Edgar K. Apgar, of Ithaca and Albany, a student of politics who had a habit of reading newspapers from all over New York State. Apgar began to follow Cleveland's career as mayor of Buffalo in the winter months of 1872, and by the spring he was writing letters to Cleveland. Apgar suggested that Cleveland seek support from the Tilden wing of the party, and Cleveland refused, for he was already a watchful and hopeful candidate for the gubernatorial nomination, who realized that in troubled waters there was good fishing, but only as long as he remained independent.

Yet Edgar Apgar was important to Cleveland's future, for he first brought the name of the Buffalo mayor into prominence in the party.

When the Democratic State Convention met in Syracuse on September 21, General Slocum and Roswell Flower were the leading candidates, as expected. Each claimed about 100 votes of a total of 385 delegates. But Cleveland had not been asleep. In Erie County he had solicited the assistance of an old friend, Tim Mahoney, and Mahoney had the Catholic vote in hand for Cleveland. Through such help, and with Cleveland's own efforts, he had some sixty votes pledged when the convention began.

That year the Republicans and Democrats met during the same week. Among the Republicans, Jay Gould, the railroad magnate, was making sure that he would control the Republican candidates in the best tradition of political bosses of the ten years just passed. Except for Tammany Hall, the Democrats immediately saw the importance of selecting an entirely different type of candidate so they could fight the election battle on the issue of machine politics. Traditionally, New York State is fairly well divided between Republicans and Democrats. The Republicans are strongest in the farm areas and in the small cities. The Democrats have always been strongest in New York City and have usually controlled the city government, and often the state government.

To win election as governor, a Democrat in New York either had to win the support of Tammany Hall, which controlled the New York City Democratic vote, or to win a great number of Republican and independent votes outside the city.

The Democratic convention was scheduled to begin on Thursday, September 21, at Syracuse. By Thursday the news about the Republican nomination of Charles J. Folger had been received, and the assembling delegates expressed their dislike for their two major candidates. Many delegates said they wanted to meet Grover Cleveland, whose name seemed to have become so prominent overnight. Cleveland obligingly took a train to Syracuse, held an open house in the lobby of a hotel where he met any and all delegates who wanted to shake his hand, and then called on Daniel Manning, the chairman of the state Democratic organization. It was two o'clock in the morning before he started back to Buffalo.

The next day, after the nominations were made, Apgar made a speech for Cleveland, pointing out the danger of selecting one of the candidates who represented one of the three wings of the party. On the third ballot, Cleveland was nominated for governor.

As was the custom at that time, the candidate, whether for governor or the Presidency of the United States, did not attend the political convention. Nor, when the convention was over, did the candidates of the two parties make many speeches themselves. The work was done by the parties.

Cleveland made no speeches at all in this campaign and did not even write any public letters, except a letter in which he accepted the nomination.

When election day came, six weeks after the nomination, Cleveland defeated his opponent by 192,000 votes out of a total of 915,000. It was the greatest victory for the Democratic party in years, and the first important victory for the Democrats since the Civil War. Even when Samuel J. Tilden had been elected governor of New York a few years before, he had won by scarcely more than fifty thousand votes. Such a large majority by a Democrat, in a period in which the Republicans controlled most states outside the south, could not help but bring Cleveland to national attention as a possible candidate for the Democratic presidential nomination in 1884.

So it was true that Cleveland, an obscure lawyer in a small New York city in 1880, became a national figure of importance two years later. The Democrats needed a leader and a symbol, and Cleveland seemed to have more promise than any other man.

But would Cleveland live up to that promise?

The answer would be found in the way he acted as governor of New York.

Cleveland indicated his policy for action before he ever moved to Albany to become governor. A few days after his election he told a friend that he had decided that he would put party considerations aside and work only for the interests of the people of the state. When he moved to Albany he threw the doors of his office wide open and did business in public, not behind locked doors. Politicians in the past had come to seek favors of other governors. Cleveland gave no such favors.

Cleveland had one great advantage when he went into office as governor: he did not owe his election to any of the three groups in the Democratic party. They needed him, if they were to have a Democratic administration, but he did not need them to hold the party together.

He was lucky in another way, too. The two houses of the New York legislature were both in the hands of the Democrats, which was not altogether usual, since the Republicans held so many votes outside New York City. But the victory of the Democrats did not mean that Governor Cleveland would have an easy time of it. The most important factor in the party, after the election, was Tammany Hall, which controlled many legislators and wanted Cleveland to appoint Tammany men to high political posts.

Cleveland made a strong reputation, from the beginning, by refusing to appoint politicians to offices just because they were Democrats, or to fire office-holders just because they were Republicans.

Many of the bills introduced in the legislature by custom were bills to benefit some small group of voters who had helped win elections, or to enrich some political leaders. For a great number of years the politicians had been using public office as a stepping stone to wealth, and where personal enrichment was not the motive, often the reason for a proposed law was to satisfy some small pressure group.

Some of the legislators proposed a bill which would allow county supervisors, all over New York State, to erect soldiers' monuments. In every county seat in New York, then, a grand pile of stone or bronze would have been put up to commemorate the men who had died for the Union in the Civil War. The results would have been handsome for the county seats, and more handsome yet for the officials and artists and manufacturers who would participate in such projects. Cleveland vetoed the bill, noting that he could not forget that the public money was raised by taxation and that tax money should not be used except for a purpose that involved the safety or welfare of the general public.

As governor of New York, Cleveland was perhaps best known, however, for his veto of what was called the Five Cent Fare Bill for New York City.

By 1883, when Cleveland became governor, New York City had developed a bustling system of elevated railroads. Jay Gould, the Republican financier and robber baron, had come into control of the elevated railroads, and he had already made a fortune from them by "stock watering," which meant simply that he had issued shares of stock to himself, and then declared the railroad's property to be more valuable than it had been the day before, although nothing at all had been added to it. The "stock watering" was a common practice of the day. Commo-

dore Vanderbilt, who owned the New York Central Railroad, had created $25 million of his fortune in a few
months by doing exactly the same.

It is easy to understand, however, that many public
spirited citizens in New York were angry with Gould.
They decided to pass a bill which would force him to
lower the fare on the elevated railroad to five cents at all
times. Tammany Hall led the fight, not because it was
particularly interested in the public welfare, but because
this support made good political talk, and, also, it wanted
to strike back at a Republican.

The Five Cent Fare Bill passed both houses of the legislature in a voice vote. It was supported by Theodore
Roosevelt, who was then the leader of the Republicans in
the Assembly, the lower house. Nonetheless, Governor
Cleveland decided he would veto the bill.

It was not a question of showing favoritism for Jay
Gould, for Grover Cleveland did not like Gould. It was
not a question of rebuking Tammany Hall, for Cleveland
had no real reason to be angry with Tammany. His veto
was prompted by a question of principle. When the street
railroads had been formed, they had been given franchises
which promised them a fair return on the money invested.
Even then, the city of New York had more need for transportation facilities, but it was difficult to find men to risk
their money in such business. If the Five Cent Fare had
become law, it might have been impossible. The bill was
unconstitutional, Cleveland argued, because the state had
a contract with each company. The fact that the companies had fallen into the hands of Jay Gould had nothing
to do with the matter.

Cleveland's position was strong, but he knew there was
a great deal of sentiment in favor of this bill, including
that of most of the New York newspapers. He signed the

veto message and went to the legislature, remarking that
night that he expected to find himself the most unpopular
man in New York on the next day.

The result was just the opposite. When the veto message was read, the legislators saw that they had been duped
by their own emotions into action that might be very
harmful to the people of the state. Tammany Hall, naturally enough, had no such compunctions, and the Tammany legislators met to consider overriding the veto. But
sentiment was changing, hour by hour. Theodore Roosevelt made a public statement that the governor was right
and that he, Roosevelt, had been wrong in supporting the
bill in the first place. A number of the New York City
newspapers, which had supported the bill originally, now
came around to Cleveland's position.

The result was that instead of becoming the most unpopular man in New York State by his veto of the fare
bill, Governor Cleveland won the respect of thousands of
people who knew very little about him, and the support
of a number of newspapers throughout the state.

As governor, Cleveland was known for his uncompromising support of the public, just as he had been known in
Buffalo. He was regarded as strong and even handsome,
although he had grown much fatter than he had been as
mayor.

Cleveland had begun to grow gray—after all he was past
forty-five years old—but he was still very strong and mas-
culine, with the heavy mustache which completely covered
his mouth and drooped slightly along the sides. His face
was firm and stern—stern with reason.

Almost from the moment that Cleveland became governor, he entered a state of siege with certain corrupt ele-
ments in the Democratic party, particularly within Tammany Hall. It began, really, in a struggle with Thomas F.

Grady, the leader of the Tammany group in the state senate.

Grady was thirty years old at this time, a stocky young man from New York City with wavy hair and blue eyes, who was serving his fifth year in the legislature in 1883. He was known in Albany as the spokesman for Honest John Kelly, the leader of Tammany Hall. He was also known for his drinking and debauchery, which sometimes kept him absent from the Senate for a week or two at a time.

Grady had a personal interest in one piece of legislation that was brought to the floor of the Senate in the legislative session of 1883. This bill would have given the Western Union Company the right to place its telegraph poles anywhere in the state, without the consent of, or without paying the owner of the property. Cleveland vetoed the bill as an improper invasion of the rights of the public, and as an excuse for corporations to seize private property. Grady was furious.

The struggle with Tammany became more serious when Honest John Kelly came up to Albany to see why the legislature was so slow in passing out political plums to Tammany's men in New York City. Particularly, Kelly was interested in two matters: the appointments to the immigration committee, which helped newly landed immigrants from foreign lands find homes and jobs; and the appointment of some two hundred harbor masters, who assigned ships to various docks and performed other duties —but were mostly noted for drawing state pay and working for Tammany Hall, which had almost always controlled the appointments.

In 1882 the four-man immigration commission had been granted $200,000 for its work, a huge sum in those days. But the money was almost completely wasted, and the immigrants, who were to benefit, more often were fleeced and mistreated by the commissioners and their hirelings.

A bill was passed to end the mistreatment of the immigrants, and Cleveland signed it. Kelly and Grady insisted that the control of the commission be placed in the hands of Tammany Hall, but Cleveland appointed William H. Murtha, a man from Brooklyn, who belonged to the Brooklyn branch of the Democratic party and not to Tammany. Grady, through his power in the Senate, refused to confirm Murtha in the job. Cleveland, on his part, refused to appoint any of the men Grady had requested for the jobs as harbor masters.

That is how matters stood on May 4th, the last day of the legislative session. Senator Grady was not worried, however. He was sure that Cleveland would capitulate to Tammany's power before the day ended, and that he would have his way on the matter of the immigration commission and the harbor masters.

Cleveland's appointment of Murtha was safely tied up in committee, and Senator Grady sat comfortably in his Senate seat, waiting for the governor to capitulate.

Just before the luncheon recess, Cleveland's secretary appeared in the Senate Chamber, and Grady waited for the secretary to come to him to tell him that Cleveland would appoint Grady's man harbor master. But the secretary paid no attention to Grady, and instead, delivered to the clerk a message from the governor—the most stinging message ever delivered to a Senate of New York State.

Cleveland reviewed the history of corruption of the immigration commission, the reasons for the change in the law, and the appointment he had made. He noted that there was no question of the fitness of Murtha, but that the appointment had simply been bottled up because of the "overwhelming greed for the patronage which may attach to the place." He called the Senate captious and noted that if the irresponsibility was not wiped out, the people must know why the legislators had failed to do their duty.

Most of the Democrats in the Senate were shamed into changing their minds, but Grady allied the Tammany men with the Republicans to stand fast against confirmation of Murtha, and the legislature adjourned without any action on the position.

Tammany did not get its jobs, and Cleveland did not get his reform of the immigration commission. It was now open warfare between Governor Cleveland and Tammany Hall.

That summer of 1883 Cleveland spent most of the days in Albany, rising at seven in the morning, and after breakfast walking the mile to the capitol from the governor's mansion. He walked home for lunch, then walked back to the office and home for dinner. And often as not, he returned to the capitol again in the evening staying until almost 1:00 A.M. working again in his office. He lived quietly, with one of his sisters as housekeeper; he got little exercise aside from walking and grew steadily fatter; and he grew tired. Once in a while, to escape the cares of office, he went fishing, either on the Hudson river or up in the Adirondack mountains. He still loved fishing and the outdoors, but his conscience invariably drove him back to the office before a vacation was well-launched.

In the fall of 1883, Cleveland wrote Boss Kelly of Tammany Hall that he did not want Senator Grady returned to office. This was drastic action, for no previous governor had attempted to dictate to the omnipotent Tammany on questions of office-holding.

The split was irreparable. Tammany hated Cleveland and Cleveland had no use for Tammany. In the elections that fall, the Republicans, strengthened by the Democratic dissension, elected majorities to both the Assembly and the state Senate. In a way this seemed disastrous, but actually, Cleveland suffered no more with a Republican legislature than he had with the Democratic legislature the previous year, and in many ways his lot was easier. Theodore Roosevelt was the leader of the Assembly's Republicans, and he and Cleveland worked together to clean up the state government—it was a partnership that was long remembered in New York State. Together, they brought through legislation which substituted the salary system for the old fee system in public offices (and saved hundreds of thousands of dollars each year for the taxpayers), legislation to give mayors power to appoint many city officials and to remove them, with the approval of the governor. They took away from the aldermen of the city of New York their power of confirming the mayor's appointments, power which had previously given the aldermen a stranglehold on the city government.

Cleveland and Roosevelt could not agree on all measures—one could not expect a Republican and a Democrat to agree so steadily—but they did work together well enough to clean up much state corruption and to install the beginnings of a civil service system in New York.

Finally, in the summer of 1884, when the Democrats made ready to go to Chicago to nominate a Presidential candidate, Grover Cleveland's name led all the others. For in his vetoes of bad legislation, his unflinching letters to the legislature, and most of all in his struggle with Tammany Hall, Cleveland had emerged as a national figure of the first importance.

CHICAGO GALOP.

GROVER CLEVELAND.

ADLAI E. STEVENSON.

BY EDUARD HOLST.

— 4 —

NEW YORK:

HITCHCOCK'S MUSIC STORES,

385 SIXTH AVENUE,

11 PARK ROW.   385 SIXTH AVENUE,

294 GRAND STREET

Chicago, Ill.: NATIONAL MUSIC CO., 215 Wabash Avenue.

SHEET MUSIC
Campaign music for the Cleveland-Stevenson ticket, 1892

Caricature: "Cleveland Wins"—1892

The President's grip; or, our infant Hercules

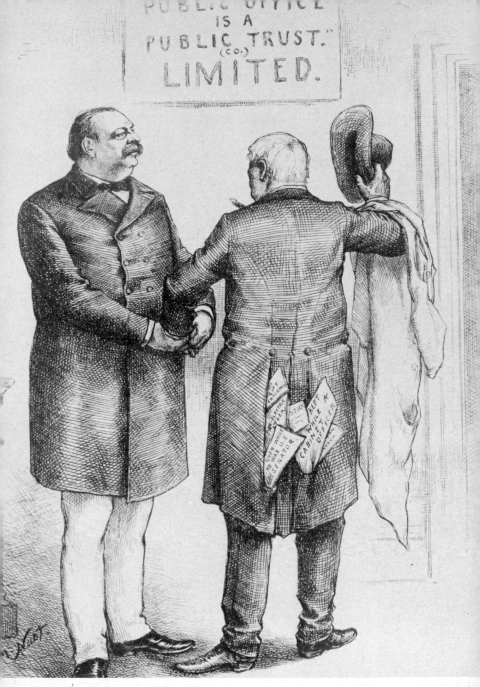

A TOO SHORT VACATION

ATTORNEY-GENERAL GARLAND. "I won't stay away long. I know how you will miss such an embodiment of your noble sentiments."

THE WATCH ON SPOILERS
Democratic tigers and Republican vultures must be kept at bay.

Mrs. Grover Cleveland in her wedding gown

AT HIS POST

PRESIDENT CLEVELAND. "I am so thoroughly tired of disapproving gifts of
public money to individuals who in my view have no right or claim to the
same, notwithstanding apparent Congressional sanction."

The wedding of Cleveland in the Blue Room of the White House

The President's wedding—the departure from the White House

☆ rum, romanism, and rebellion

AMONG THE financial panics which have ravaged the American business community over the years, the one which occurred in May, 1884, is particularly notable because it destroyed the fortune of Ulysses Simpson Grant, the general and former President who had gone into business in Wall Street as an investment banker.

Grant's political fortunes had been wiped out a decade before, and yet even in 1884, nearly twenty years after the end of the Civil War, northern politicians nominated generals and still tried to raise the spectre of revolution. If the Democrats were elected to control Congress and the White House, the Republicans charged, they would encourage the southern states to rebel again and the Civil War would have to be fought a second time.

This nonsense had been effective in every political campaign since 1864 (a year in which there was some reason for distrust of Democratic policy) Yet by 1884 enough time had elapsed and enough new problems had been added to American politics so that the biennial cries of the Republicans about the war would go unheeded. The voters were tired of hearing about the Civil War and they were much more concerned about the general air of dishonesty which seemed to hang over all kinds of government.

Since the beginning of the Civil War, people in the north had grown used to dishonesty in government, although they were never entirely comfortable in hearing about it. There was so much dishonesty in the business world and such outrageous use of power by industrialists that this age is often referred to as the Era of the Robber Barons. Jay Gould, Commodore Vanderbilt, Jim Fiske, Leland Stanford—these and scores of other men created huge fortunes. They did not hesitate to buy and sell legislators, and the legislators were so easily bribed that everyone in America was aware of the corruption. Late in the 1860's, Boss Tweed of New York claimed to have bribed all the members of the New York State Senate except one. A few years later the Crédit Mobilier scandal broke, a disgrace which involved the company organized to finance the building of the Union Pacific railroad. The Crédit Mobilier scandal reached high into the government. Schuyler Colfax, Vice-President of the United States, was one of the men who had accepted a bribe from the industrialists who wanted favors and huge grants of public land for their railroad company.

It was a strange period, this postwar interlude of thievery. American regard for morality was very low, particularly for morality in government. Yet the common people, whose one weapon was their vote, were dissatisfied with this kind of government by evil, and from time to time they rose against it. Once a man went too far he destroyed himself, for the average Americans would eventually throw him out. Both political parties were involved in dishonesties, and in various sections of the country there was not much choice between them. Both parties bought votes, stuffed ballot boxes, and cheated on election returns when they thought they could get away with it. Still, the politicians knew they would have to answer to the voters, and that they could not fool them forever. So Schuyler Colfax, once his dishonesty had been uncovered, saw his political career destroyed. Boss Tweed, who rose from poverty to become the third largest holder of real estate in New York City, fled to Spain with his wealth, was captured and brought back to America, and died in jail.

By 1884 the workers and farmers of the United States were sick of reading in their newspapers about corruption in government. Not everyone in America felt so strongly, but beneath the surface of American life the current of a revived interest in high moral standards was moving swiftly. There could hardly be a better illustration of the movement than the career of Grover Cleveland: his first important public office, that of sheriff of Erie County, came during the early postwar years, when neither he nor anyone else, it appeared, was particularly conscious of the evils in the loose system of government. As sheriff, Cleveland made a substantial amount of money through the fees he collected for doing his duty; it was a system under which public officials did not receive salaries, and thus a system that made every public official a target for bribery and temptation.

A few years later, however, Grover Cleveland had developed genuine concern for good government, for he had seen so much corruption and bribery around him. As mayor of Buffalo, Cleveland was notable for his strength of character and his honesty, and as he exhibited those characteristics, the people of Buffalo cheered and their faith was lifted, for Cleveland was proving to them that decent government was possible. As when a stone is dropped into a placid pond, the wave of faith and indignation widened. Cleveland was not the only honest mayor in America, and it would be incorrect to say that the resurgence of morality in American government all began in

Buffalo. It did not. Simultaneously, citizens in other communities and other states were feeling the same revulsion against boss rule and cheap politics. But through a combination of circumstances, strength of character, and good luck, Grover Cleveland had been elected governor of New York.

Once again there was opportunity for him to fail miserably. He could have succumbed to the corrupt Senator Grady and the bosses of Tammany Hall; or he could have sought only public popularity by passing all measures that seemed to favor the common people and vetoing others. Cleveland did not do so. His veto of the Five Cent Fare Bill was typically courageous—he vetoed a bill that *seemed* to favor the common people because he believed it was unconstitutional. This solidity, this strength of character, was something the people could understand, and whether or not they agreed with the man, they respected him for it —except, of course, those in his own party and those out of it whose toes he stepped on.

By the time the Democrats of the nation trouped to Chicago in the summer of 1884 for their national convention, the Republicans had already met in that city and had chosen James Gillespie Blaine as their nominee for the Presidency.

Blaine was fifty-four years old, and most of his adult years had been spent in government. He had been a member of the House of Representatives from Maine. Later he had been chosen Speaker of the House. He had been elected Senator from Maine, and had left the Senate to become Secretary of State in the cabinet of James Garfield, a prize awarded him because of his own narrow defeat for the Republican nomination in 1880. When Garfield was assassinated a few weeks after his inauguration, Blaine resigned from the cabinet. He had been living as a private citizen, in Washington and Maine, conducting private business and waiting for his chance to get back into politics.

Blaine had been involved in the Crédit Mobilier scandal —although his misdoing was minor, if serious at all. He had also been involved in using his official position to help various railroads and other businesses in which he had a personal interest. Until after he had become deeply involved in such practices, apparently Blaine had seen nothing wrong in mixing public and private business, and using his position for personal profit. It was common practice in the easy climate of the post-war years, and it only became a serious offense when exposed in the 1870's, after a number of scandals had made the public realize that many officials were stealing the taxpayers' money. It was impossible to undo what had been done, so Blaine did the next best thing, he tried to conceal his record of mixing public and private affairs.

He had concealed it enough to secure the Republican nomination before the Democrats assembled in Chicago in July, but not enough to keep the Republican party from splitting. A group of important Republican leaders announced that they could not support Blaine. If the Democrats brought forth a candidate they believed to be honest and able, these men said, they would support the Democrats.

When Cleveland's supporters from upstate New York arrived in Chicago, they found that Tammany Hall had sent its delegates before them. Thomas Grady, Cleveland's old enemy, was in the city, bribing newspaper reporters and buying drinks for anyone he might convince that Cleveland was dishonest, inept, and a drunkard besides.

Before the convention began, six hundred men from Tammany Hall arrived in Chicago with the single aim of stopping Cleveland's nomination for President.

Why was Tammany so anxious to stop Cleveland if Boss Kelly had no candidate of his own? In the first place, Cleveland had already shown how he felt about doing favors for political henchmen, and Tammany Hall existed on favors and bribery. In the second place, if Cleveland were nominated, Tammany Hall would lose its place as the foremost Democratic organization in New York. Tammany's place had been threatened by the Tilden organization, but Tilden was now old and infirm. He declined even to have his name mentioned for the Presidency in 1884 and let his organization support Cleveland's candidacy. Tammany Hall was determined to stop Cleveland and thus retain control of the Democratic organization of the entire state. Even if a Republican administration were elected to office, Boss Kelly thought that a small price to pay, as long as he could consolidate his own power.

Tammany's first move was to try to amend what is called "the unit rule," under which Democratic conventions worked. Under the "unit rule" the delegates from each state held a meeting (caucus) before the nominations were made. Then the delegates voted for the candidates they preferred; the votes were counted; and the candidate who received a majority would then be the candidate of the state—every delegate's vote would be cast for that one man.

Tammany Hall, of course, realized that the combined strength of all the other Democratic groups in New York would force the Tammany men to support Cleveland, although they hated him. If they could change the convention rules, they could keep from voting for Cleveland and help defeat him.

Grady got up on the convention floor during the first session of the convention and proposed that the rule be changed. The amendment was defeated by 463 votes to 332. Cleveland's backers had won the first round of the fight, but the battle was not over.

"I will not lift a hand to help him," said Boss Kelly, when asked what he was going to do for Cleveland. That was not the entire story, however. Kelly went much further; he and his Tammany men spent hours in saloons and smoke-filled rooms, doing everything they could with other delegations to try to stop Cleveland.

Boss Kelly went to meet with General Benjamin Butler, who had been elected governor of Massachusetts in 1882 and this year had already been nominated for the Presidency as the candidate of the Anti-Monopolist and Greenback parties—two small groups whose names indicated the feeling in favor of reform that was growing across the country. That night Kelly and Butler planned a demonstration at the convention in favor of Thomas A. Hendricks of Indiana, a candidate who had been nominated and had received a single vote.

On the third day of the convention, when the voting began, Cleveland had received 392 votes, twice as many as his nearest rival, Thomas Bayard, but still not enough for victory, for under the convention rules he must receive two-thirds of all the votes cast.

Kelly agreed to work for Hendricks so he could defeat Cleveland; Butler had another reason: he hoped that if Cleveland's chances failed, then the Cleveland backers would come around and support him—Butler—as a compromise candidate for the nomination.

Boss Kelly and General Butler bribed the sergeant at arms of the convention, and he allowed them to pack the galleries with men who were instructed to start cheering and stamping their feet as soon as Hendricks' name was mentioned. But Tammany was not to have so easy a victory.

By this time, the entire convention was aware of the struggle between Grover Cleveland and Tammany Hall. Cleveland could not have had better publicity, for the Democrats were sick of Tammany Hall, which never failed to trade votes with the Republicans of New York if Tammany's power could thus be increased. Tammany had predicted the defeat of Tilden in New York in 1876 and had not worked for him—yet Tilden had won New York. Tammany had betrayed General Hancock in the election of 1880 to strengthen its position in the state. The Democrats at the convention did not forget that, and when Grady had jumped up during the convention to shout that Cleveland could not carry the state of New York, he was booed into silence.

A little later, General Edward Bragg of Wisconsin arose and turned on Tammany Hall. "They love Cleveland for his character," he said about the governor of New York, "but they love him also for the enemies he has made."

So while Boss Kelly and General Butler schemed to arrange a "spontaneous demonstration" for Hendricks, others at the convention discovered the plot and sent messages around to every delegation informing them of the plan.

The next day, when Hendricks entered the hall and the shouting and stamping began, the delegates just sat there and looked at the galleries and at Tammany Hall, whose members were shouting and screaming and waving their arms. The demonstration was a failure; Tammany had lost. On the second ballot Cleveland was nominated, and the election campaign of 1884 began.

When the nomination came, Cleveland was working in

his office in Albany, and he neither stopped working that day, nor seemed in any way elated or emotionally aroused by the event. Calmly, in the manner people had grown to expect from him, he continued to do his job as chief executive of the state of New York.

The election campaign of 1884 was remembered for many years, not because of the issues between the two parties—because scarcely anyone could remember the issues in later years—but because of the two men. Blaine and Cleveland, they became the issues, and from the very beginning the real question was the question of morality.

A few days after the Democratic convention, a group of prominent Republicans announced their support of Cleveland. They called themselves Independent Republicans, but the rest of the world called them Mugwumps—a corruption of an Indian word *mugquomp*, which meant chief. The other Republicans chose that term in derision of the Independents, because they said the Independents thought themselves too good for common Republicans.

The Mugwumps raised the moral issues almost immediately, linking Blaine with the Crédit Mobilier scandal and charging that he had taken stock in the Little Rock and Fort Smith Railroad as a bribe.

In the beginning the Republicans did not know how to respond to these charges, although Blaine hated to be on the defensive and tried to rally the party to discuss the tariff. But who wanted to talk about the tariff, when they could talk about whether or not one of the candidates was an honest man?

The Republicans tried to bring up the Civil War again; Republican newspapers and Republican speakers discussed the threat of the "solid south" to the nation and recalled the blood and expense of the rebellion, as though the Democratic party alone were responsible for these evils. But the voters were not listening to such talk this year.

Late in July the Republicans thought they had found an issue that would help them and counter the arguments about Blaine's honesty. A scurrilous Buffalo newspaper, the *Evening Telegraph,* printed a story about Cleveland's liaison with Maria Halpin, adding many details which were not true and indicating that Cleveland was habitually immoral.

All across the country the Republican newspapers seized on this story to retaliate for the charges made against Blaine. Two Buffalo ministers seized this chance to become nationally famous and to strike blows for religious purity—by attacking Cleveland without investigating the charges. These attacks provided more fuel for the Republicans until Henry Ward Beecher, the great preacher of the day, and Dr. James Freeman Clarke, the famous minister of Boston, investigated the charges and announced their faith in Cleveland. It was true that Cleveland had been involved with Mrs. Halpin, but after the initial mistake he had behaved better than might be expected, and the ministers felt that no man could be forever chastised for a human mistake which he had done all possible to rectify.

Some voters were torn between the claims that Cleveland had been privately immoral and Blaine had been publicly dishonest. A Chicago man summed up the problem when he said that since Blaine had been delinquent in public life but blameless in private life, and Cleveland had been blameless in public life but delinquent in private life, Cleveland ought to be elected and Blaine ought to be returned to private life, so each could fill the station for which he was best qualified.

It was a good joke, but it did not convince many people, one way or another. What did happen was that the question of morality, public and private, kept growing in importance during the campaign.

Cleveland was the best behaved of all the politicians. His friends went too far in his defense, and his enemies went too far in trying to ruin him. Cleveland stayed in Albany, minding his business and refusing to be drawn into a game of name-calling.

"Whatever you do, tell the truth," Cleveland said to his assistants and campaign workers.

A new series of letters which linked Blaine with corruption was uncovered during the campaign, and it did much to take the minds of Democrats off the Halpin affair. Blaine had written an associate regarding some business dealings and then had told him to burn the letter. Why, asked the nation, should the letter be burned if there was nothing wrong?

One time, Cleveland supporters brought a package of what they called evidence about wrongdoing in Blaine's private life and placed it on the governor's desk in Albany.

"Are all the papers here?" Cleveland, asked, and when he was told they were in the package, he calmly tore the papers up, threw them in a wastebasket, and watched while a servant burned the papers in a fireplace. "The other side can have a monopoly of all the dirt in this campaign," he said.

Boss Kelly of Tammany Hall did not know what to do in this campaign. He hoped, almost until the last, that Cleveland would be forced to withdraw by the scandal about his private life. In September, however, Kelly came to the conclusion that unless he supported the national ticket, Tammany might be ruined, for its stock within the

Democratic party was low enough already. He turned to
lukewarm support of Cleveland.

Until the end of the campaign, the outcome was in
doubt. Cleveland had been hurt by the revelation of the
Halpin story, but Blaine had been hurt more severely by
the disclosure of his untidy official life. Cleveland made
only two speeches during the campaign, but Blaine, feeling the need for explanation, took to the campaign trail;
particularly, he was persuaded to travel to the west, where
Republican fortunes seemed very shaky.

There were many side issues in the campaign. Catholics
were convinced that Cleveland was anti-Catholic and that
Blaine, whose mother had been a Catholic, favored them;
but the church hierarchy was annoyed that the religious
issue should be interjected, and Cleveland came to suspect
that it had done him as much good as it did harm.

On October 29, Cleveland was proved right. When
Blaine arrived in New York City, tired from his western
trip, he was greeted by a delegation of Protestant clergymen, who referred to the Democratic party as the party of
"Rum, Romanism, and Rebellion." Because of Tammany
Hall's lukewarm support, Blaine had hoped to attract much
of the Irish Catholic vote, traditionally Democratic, which
was located in the big cities of the east. The Irish usually
looked to the Irishmen of Tammany for guidance. But
with that statement of the clergymen, which Blaine did not
disavow, the Catholics turned against Blaine.

Further, on the same evening, Blaine attended a ban-
quet at Delmonico's Restaurant. The party had been arranged by the Republicans for two hundred industrial
leaders, to present Blaine and then try to squeeze campaign contributions from them. The next day the Democratic newspapers of New York linked Blaine with Jay
Gould, John Jacob Astor, Cyrus Field, and dozens of other

millionaires, making it appear that if he were elected the poor would starve in rags, while Blaine feasted with the rich.

Then, most disastrous of all for Blaine, on election day it rained, which meant that many farmers would not get to the polls and many Republican votes would be lost. It was a close election. The results were unknown for three days, and the Republican New York *Tribune* claimed that Blaine had been elected. But on the Saturday after the election it became known that Cleveland had carried New York (by less than 1200 votes) and New York was decisive. Cleveland had won the southern states, and he had carried Indiana, New Jersey, and Connecticut. He was elected President of the United States.

☆ the businessman's president

ON THE DAY that he was elected President of the United States, Grover Cleveland was admittedly one of the least informed men in the nation on the problems that faced the American people. While he tried to inform himself as much as possible in the few short months between election and inauguration, he still had a full time job as governor of New York until the first of January, 1885.

In those days the Presidential term began in March of the year following election. Fortunately, then, Cleveland had two months of relative leisure in which to study the most serious issues and select his cabinet.

On one major issue he was well-informed, and that was the problem of patronage—the privilege of government jobs for the party workers who had supported him.

In the second half of the twentieth century, when the vast majority of federal government employees are protected by the Civil Service laws, it is hard to understand the difficulties Grover Cleveland faced. When he was elected, there were 126,000 federal employees, and of these only 16,000 were protected by the infant Civil Service system. In other words, Grover Cleveland, directly and indirectly, had to be responsible for decisions on 110,000 jobs. Since the Republicans had been in control of the Presidency steadily for more than twenty years, nearly all those jobs were held by Republicans. The Democrats, who had controlled just a few state administrations, were hungry for federal jobs and determined to have them. But at the same time, the Independent Republicans who had supported Cleveland, and some Democrats, urged the newly elected President to extend the Civil Service and refuse to fire employees just because they were Republicans.

The regular party workers detested these independents, who wanted to change the old system under which the party in power grew fat, while the politicians out of power struggled. To show how strongly the local politicians felt it was only necessary to recall that President Garfield's assassin was an office seeker who had not been appointed to the job he wanted.

Grover Cleveland sympathized with the reformers who wanted to end the evils of constant office-changing and to persuade better men to make a career of government. Even before his inauguration he had pledged to uphold the Civil Service Law of 1883, which protected some employees. Now Cleveland went even further and announced that he would not remove men, even though they were not under Civil Service, just because they were Republicans. He would remove the Republicans who had been extremely partisan in the campaign, and he would remove inefficient employees, whether they were Republican or Democrat. In that statement Cleveland served notice on both Republicans and Democrats that ability and honesty would be the signs he would look for in making his decisions about public office.

The Democrats who were familiar with Cleveland's record expected him to take this attitude towards government jobs, but that did not prevent hundreds of men, from Congressmen to ward leaders, from coming to Cleveland's

office in Albany, trying to persuade him to appoint them
or their relatives or friends to some post.

In February, Cleveland travelled to New York City,
stayed at the Victoria Hotel, and for three days did little
else but interview people who wanted jobs.

After his inauguration on March 4, the horde of job-
hunters increased. Cleveland was to learn that dozens of
his friends—or men he had believed to be his friends—
were now demanding government positions. When they
did not get what they wanted, they turned against him.

For example, one old crony of Cleveland's was a German
named George Gruener, of Buffalo. Gruener owned a
restaurant where Cleveland had often gone to eat and
drink and in the years when Cleveland lived in Buffalo,
Gruener had been one of his companions at cards. After
the election, Gruener decided that he would become
either postmaster of Buffalo or Collector of Customs for
the port. He went to Washington to tell Cleveland what
he wanted. When he arrived, Cleveland greeted him as a
friend, but when Gruener did not get either job, he turned
against the President.

Another man from Buffalo wrote the new President a
letter asking for a job, and without waiting for a reply
moved his family to Washington. Cleveland was angry
and upset, and he wrote to friends in Buffalo urging them
to stop the office-seekers from coming to Washington.

Cleveland's old friend and law partner, Wilson Bissell,
hoped to become a member of the cabinet, or at least an
ambassador, but when the appointments were made, he
received neither job. Cleveland was trying hard to make
his appointments serve the nation, not his friends. Bissell
was wounded, and for some months there was a coolness
in their relations.

But President Cleveland was pressed harder by political acquaintances than he was ever pressed by his friends. Honest John Kelly, the boss of Tammany Hall who had supported Cleveland so reluctantly, wanted a Tammany man appointed to the most important postmastership in America—that of New York City.

The job had been held by Henry G. Pearson, a Republican, who had done so good a job of administering the largest post office in the country that many Democrats approved of him. Cleveland, true to his own word to keep efficient men in office, no matter what their politics, reappointed Pearson postmaster and asked the U. S. Senate to confirm the appointment, as he did with almost all political appointments under the law. Boss Kelly was furious, but the appointment was made anyway.

By appointing two former Confederate soldiers to his cabinet, Cleveland brought the south back into the national government on an entirely equal basis for the first time since the secession of the Confederate states. But even southern Senators and Congressmen became angry with the President because he would not yield to their demands for appointment of their friends and party workers.

It is sometimes said Cleveland's administration came at a quiet time when no important issues faced the United States; that he had no positive program to offer; and that his sole purpose was to give Americans an efficient and honest government. The problem with this kind of an interpretation of history is that it gives, in hindsight, a great number of Presidents of the United States credit for having anticipated the problems of the day and having come into office with detailed plans for solving them. The fact is that almost all Presidents of the United States felt their

way, and that most great decisions and government programs were the result of trial and error. The unfortunate
impression is that Grover Cleveland's first administration
was a period of dull tranquility, marked only by his struggle with office-seekers, his efforts to pull the nation out
of depression, and changes in his personal life.

But the first Cleveland administration was marked by
much change, at home and abroad. Britain was extending
her empire to Africa, moving from both north and south.
In 1885, before Cleveland took office, General "Chinese"
Gordon was killed at Khartoum and the British garrison
in the Sudan was wiped out. China and Japan struggled
over the future of Korea. The French moved in on Indo-
China. Germany annexed the Marshall and Solomon
islands. It was an age of imperialism, and the course of
American policy was to affect the ambitions of the rulers
of Europe. The United States was still an isolated nation,
suspicious and fearful of Europe and European quarrels,
but we were not living in a vacuum, even then, and we
were involved in the intrigues of European courts,
whether we liked it or not. Grover Cleveland's appointments, especially to the diplomatic corps, were to have
serious effects on the future of American foreign relations,
and even on internal politics.

Early in his administration, Cleveland appointed a
Catholic from Virginia named Anthony M. Keiley as minister to Italy. Keiley had long been interested in international affairs, but unfortunately he was an outspoken
man. Fourteen years before his appointment, Keiley had
made a speech protesting the separation of the Catholic
church from the Italian state, and challenging the authority of the civil authorities in Italy. He was a good Catholic, but when a newspaper dug up the story of the old
speech, suddenly the Italian foreign office refused to accept

Keiley's credentials as ambassador. This action brought up the religious issue in America and abroad. An American Catholic archbishop, who had recommended Keiley for the post, was embarrassed and angry. Catholics were annoyed, and so were anti-Catholics. Cleveland was in a most difficult position.

He tried to escape embarrassment by appointing Keiley ambassador to the court of Franz Joseph, the emperor of Austria-Hungary, and leaped squarely into the middle of complicated European politics. The Austro-Hungarian empire and Italy were in constant dispute over that mixed area north and east of the Adriatic Sea which has changed hands many times in modern history. If the court at Vienna accepted Keiley, after Italy had rejected him, it would appear to be an affront to the Italian government by Franz Joseph. Further, Keiley was married to a Jew, and the Viennese court was not pleased. The issue was made, by the Austro-Hungarian foreign office, on the Jewish question. Cleveland was so angry he withdrew the appointment—but refused to appoint any ambassador to Austria-Hungary.

Cleveland recognized, from the first, that his most important job was to bring good government to the United States, and that this could be done only by reform of the entire process of administration. The reform-minded, chief of whom was Carl Schurz, an independent Republican from Missouri, were concerned almost entirely with the elimination of the old spoils system, which had flourished under Grant and his successors, at least until the administration of President Arthur. Whole departments of government had to be rebuilt from top to bottom, starting with new cabinet officers. William C. Whitney, the Secretary of the Navy, discovered that while the United States government had spent twenty-five million dollars since 1868 on ships, seventy million dollars of that amount had been wasted. When Secretary Whitney went into office, the United States did not have a single warship which could have been kept at sea for a week. America did not even manufacture all its own parts but was dependent on Germany and England for certain gun parts and armor plate.

Secretary Whitney was asked to accept delivery of a steel ship which had been built under the Arthur administration. On inspection, Whitney discovered that the ship was useless. Her one useful gun was placed so it could not fire directly forward; the ship leaked; and her bow could not stand heavy seas. Even more important, Whitney learned that while England and Germany and France had progressed in conversion of their navies from wood to steel ships, the United States was far behind. Whitney began the long and difficult task of building a Navy, starting with nearly nothing at all—for no American steel mill had experience in making ship's plates.

Since the days of the War of 1812 very few Americans had been interested in naval affairs. The military campaigns of later years, fought against Indian tribes, against the Mexicans, and against the Confederacy, were almost entirely land wars. North and South had their raiders, chasers, and blockade runners during the Civil War, but they were few. When the Union had wanted to move troops to New Orleans early in the war, the government had been forced to lease ships under charter from private shipowners such as Commodore Vanderbilt and George Law.

Grover Cleveland, then, was the President who began the long process of rebuilding the United States Navy. He had no idea of turning the Navy into a primary force for war, but with three coastlines to defend and the American commitment to defense of Latin America (The Monroe Doctrine), Cleveland saw that an effective Navy was necessary.

Cleveland was known as the "businessman's President," largely because of his sympathy towards the affairs of business in America, but it is not generally known that Cleveland also set out to right some of the wrongs of previous administrations in which industrialists and capitalists had robbed the public. In particular, this had been done through turning over thousands of miles of publicly owned land to railroads as land grants. The idea behind the land grants was that the railroads needed government help to finance construction, and it was in the public interest to push railroads across the continent as quickly as possible. The principle could be defended, but not the practice—under which dozens of railroads raided the public lands and in their wake came hundreds of other businessmen, including the owners of huge cattle and sheep ranches, who staked off the public lands, fenced them, and used them as their own. Others, especially logging companies, stripped public lands of their woods. Grover Cleveland, in his first administration, laid the groundwork for the far better known conservation policies of Theodore Roosevelt. Cleveland quickly began to recover the lands that had been misappropriated and misused by the wealthy. He was the first President to establish a policy of protection for the Indians, who were constantly being squeezed onto reservations where they watched the white men grabbing their tribal lands and resources.

The reputation of this first administration as a "business" administration, then, came largely through the efforts of Daniel Manning, the Tilden leader who had been New York State Democratic chairman and who became Secretary of the Treasury in the Cleveland cabinet.

But the outstanding problems of his first term, which affected the business community so sharply and colored the entire national and historic view of his administration —these were not to come for two years.

His most important move in foreign affairs was the reversal of a Republican policy regarding the building of a canal across Central America. In the 1850's Commodore Cornelius Vanderbilt had proposed just such a canal, but the Clayton-Bulwer treaty with England had provided that neither the United States nor England would build a canal without the agreement of the other, and the English were slow to act. The Republicans under the Arthur administration had decided to go ahead and build a canal. Cleveland's election stopped it, because he refused to violate the treaty. Thus rebuffed, the Republicans, who controlled the Senate, tried to strike back at Cleveland by exerting every power the Senate had, and some it did not have, to control appointments by the President to public office. The battle was fought through most of 1885 and into the summer of 1886, before President Cleveland finally won control of appointments and caused the repeal of a hampering piece of legislation called the Tenure of Office Act which the Republicans had passed in an effort to retain control of government jobs.

As in Albany, Cleveland worked hard and played hard; the latter, however, infrequently. He rose at eight o'clock in the morning, had his breakfast, and was in the executive office on the second floor of the White House by nine o'clock. He worked until 1:30, met the general public for half an hour to shake hands and chat, and lunched at two o'clock. After lunch he went back to the office, worked almost until dinner time, and then went back to work in the library until one or two o'clock in the morning. It was often said in Washington that Cleveland worked harder and longer than any other President since James

Polk, and it was known that Polk had actually killed himself with overwork.

All the desk work did not help control Cleveland's growing portliness. He had come into office at two hundred and forty pounds, and he gained weight. His exercise, what there was of it, consisted in driving out in a carriage for fresh air and then dismounting to walk beside the carriage. Once a year, and sometimes a bit oftener, he went out for a fishing vacation. In the summer of 1885 the vacation was in the Adirondack mountains, but Cleveland seemed to spend as much time there eating, drinking, and sitting around telling stories as in casting a line.

In Washington, the President did little but work. Usually one of his sisters was staying at the White House as official hostess, but except for a few personal friends who were invited to the residence to stay from time to time, Cleveland did very little entertaining; just as he had preferred work to parties when in Albany, so he preferred to spend his time on the problems of the whole nation when in Washington. The nation did not know, however, that for two years Grover Cleveland had been secretly engaged to be married.

The secret was well kept because the girl Cleveland had chosen for his wife was Frances Folsom, the daughter of his old friend from Buffalo who had died in the carriage accident. For years, as executor of the Folsom estate, Cleveland had looked after his friend's widow and daughter. When he had gone to Albany, they had been among the guests at the executive mansion. He had followed Frances' career through school and had sent her flowers from time to time—yet in all these matters one might have supposed he was acting the part of an indulgent uncle. She was, after all, a quarter of a century younger than Cleveland.

The secret was well kept until the spring of 1886, when

Frances and her mother were travelling in Europe. In April the newspapers printed rumors, and in May the rumors grew in strength and number, but it was not until May 28 that the White House confirmed the fact. The couple was married on June 2 in the White House.

Then came the honeymoon—which turned out to be a nightmare. Grover and Frances Cleveland went by special train to Deer Park, Maryland, but almost immediately were besieged by a pack of newspaper reporters who pried into every aspect of the honeymoon (as reporters still do) hoping to find in every gesture the raw material for a news story for their newspapers. Cleveland was disgusted enough to complain and began a running battle with the sensational press, which began to harass him.

With marriage, Cleveland's life changed, for Frances Cleveland liked parties and receptions. He became more relaxed, and he was induced to work a little less hard than before, to take longer vacations, and to enjoy himself.

But in that spring of 1886, while he was preparing for his marriage, Cleveland was beginning to take an interest in a knotty problem which had bothered Presidents and Congressmen for a hundred years—the tariff—a tax on goods imported into the United States from foreign countries.

A tariff, of sorts, had been instrumental in bringing on the American Revolution, but after the colonies became a nation and had the responsibility for providing for their own taxation, the tariff issue went unresolved.

In the beginning, tariffs were put on imported goods to raise money for operation of the federal government. But there was never any real agreement between those who traded abroad and those who sold manufactures at home. The businessmen who bought goods from abroad wanted low tariffs, because if we had high tariffs on imported goods, other nations would respond with high taxes on the goods we sent abroad. Those who manufactured goods, such as shoes and clothing and machinery, wanted taxes on foreign goods of that type, because then their goods could be sold at cheaper prices.

The battle had begun with the infant Republic. By 1833 the tariff issue had been compromised so that tariffs were reduced gradually on a number of items over a nine year period. This was possible because the United States was still an importing nation, and much of the money needed to run the government could be raised by the sale of government lands in the west. During the Civil War tariffs were raised, for the growth of manufacturing in the United States had brought about a new feeling about the tariff—it was not only to be an instrument for raising money to operate the government, but was also to become a device for the protection of American industry against foreign competition. In the twenty years of Republican rule after the Civil War, the high tariff became established as a basic part of the Republican philosophy of government.

That is not to say that the Democrats were in favor of "free trade"—or no tariff at all—because, aside from a group of idealists, no one in America seriously thought in terms of free trade.

The basis for the high tariff rates that existed in 1885 had been the need to raise revenue to prosecute the war. After the war was ended, some manufacturers found the tariff so convenient in assuring their own profits on goods which were also made abroad, that they exerted every possible influence to keep tariff rates high. In consequence, some items manufactured in the United States sold for more money in this country than they sold for abroad. The abuses of the tariff system were numerous, and sometimes seemed to outweigh the honest protection afforded legitimate manufacturers against cut-rate prices from abroad.

By the time Cleveland came to the Presidency there was another problem in sight. For several years the high tariffs had brought in great amounts of revenue, and the federal treasury was overflowing. What this meant, in short, was that too much of the money in circulation was in the hands of the government. Prices had fallen, the country was in a depression; but the tariff rates remained high, and farmers and small businessmen suffered by paying high prices for the goods they needed, while the industrialists of the east made fortunes on overpriced manufactured goods.

There were tariffs on iron, on rope, on wire, on almost everything imaginable; the list was long and the rates were complicated. But the amounts of money involved were huge: in the steel industry alone the unfair profits of manufacturers were estimated at five dollars a ton, simply because of the tariff which kept British steel out of the United States.

The Democratic platform of 1884 had pledged to do something to help reform the high tariff rates, and in 1885, Cleveland asked Congress to fulfill the promise. But the Republicans and some Democrats from industrial states combined to kill the amendments to the law that year. In 1886, Cleveland again argued that the tariff must be amended, and in that year the federal surplus again rose, but once again Congress refused to act. This time Cleveland was truly angry. He threatened to call a special session of Congress to deal with the tariff arose, and he made ready for a battle on which he was prepared to stake his political future.

✧ the campaign of 1888

THE POLITICAL CAMPAIGN of 1888 in effect started for President Cleveland a year ahead of time, when he came to realize the danger of letting the system of high tariffs remain unchanged. It may seem odd that such a complicated and apparently dull economic problem would decide the election, but when the long phrases and big words were removed, the tariff issue could be translated into terms of the meat on the table in the home of a steel worker in Pittsburgh, or the new diamond necklace for Mrs. Morgan or Mrs. Carnegie.

In 1887, two years after President Cleveland had taken office, he seemed to be in an almost impregnable position. His administration was extremely popular with the people, all over the United States. The Republicans were gloomy about the prospects of defeating this big man in the elections of 1888, for he had destroyed the spoils system, the depression had ended, and the Republicans had run out of national leaders. James G. Blaine, unhappy over his narrow defeat, had gone to Europe for a long stay, and no one knew when, or if, he would be coming home.

The Democrats were complacent enough in 1887, although they were annoyed with Cleveland because he had so staunchly resisted their demands that federal jobs be put in the hands of the politicians. Cleveland had actually compromised a great deal on the issue of political patronage. He had been forced to compromise by the very nature of American politics, for political organizations can exist only if the people who work in politics feel that they can somehow, sometime, be rewarded for their efforts. Only so many people can run for Congress, or the state legislature, or even local office. Others must be rewarded, if at all, by appointed jobs, and if all the appointed jobs were to be made under the merit system, and if the jobholders were then protected against removal by the opposition party when it came to power, the vigor of the political parties would soon be lost. The Democrats made Cleveland understand the truth of this contention; he did understand it, and while he remained firm about appointing men of merit, he did make appointments on a political basis, and he did not keep Republicans in office when Democrats could do the job as well.

If President Cleveland had thought only in terms of politics he would have had no trouble in being elected again in 1888, for his administration was able, and the Republicans would have been hard pressed to find a candidate with more popular appeal than Cleveland. The President, however, was noted for a quality the New York Democrats had earlier called "ugly honesty." He was frank, he was brutal, and he came straight to the point when he saw and understood a governmental problem, without regard for the political implications.

Early in 1887 the federal government surplus began to raise problems in the American business world. In 1886 the federal government spent about two hundred and fifty million dollars, but the government collected, in taxes, almost a hundred million dollars more than it spent. In business, the excess money would be profits and would enrich the businessman, but government is not business. When the businessman accumulates extra money, he invests it, and the money then goes into the banks, or directly into other businesses. The businessman's money, in other words, is always in circulation, ready for use to keep the processes of producing and selling and buying at work. When government accumulated extra money, however, that money was not available for the business world. The government did not then lend money to private business; the government did not invest in business; so, in 1886 nearly a hundred million dollars was taken out of the business world and stored away in the federal treasury.

The effect of this money shortage was direct and immediate. Most of the money came from tariffs, which meant that the people who actually bought and used cotton, and shoes, and laces, and other goods from abroad paid the money into the treasury, when they might have been using it to buy other goods, or might be putting the money into banks. The bankers found that they did not have as much money to lend as they needed, so they were more cautious than usual in making loans, and, since their money was so much in demand, they charged higher rates of interest, which again took money out of the hands of consumers—the people who bought goods and used them.

If Congress had been truly extravagant, and had set out to spend all the money that came in, such extravagance would have created political issues, but the money would have been kept in circulation and the economy would not have suffered. No political party, except the radical third parties, had any idea of creating massive programs of public works, or of letting government actually build or produce. The government, as President Cleveland and nearly all others saw it then, was a referee, not a participant in the affairs of the nation.

There were only a few things the government could do to keep the extra money out of the treasury, given such a philosophy. Secretary Manning and President Cleveland agreed that the federal government would retire all the bonds possible. In 1886 the Treasury bought fifty million dollars worth of bonds, and more than twice that amount in 1887, but this could not go on, because by retiring the government bonds, the Treasury dried up one investment opportunity for the people; each bond retired meant the federal government stopped paying that much interest.

For months, President Cleveland and his assistants tried to find solutions to the problem. Secretary Manning wanted to retire the country's paper money. Still another official suggested that the treasury lend the money to the banks; but the country had found paper money to be a great convenience, and Congress was not willing to accept government participation in business, even the banking business. In the end, nothing was done, and the surplus kept piling up in the Treasury.

In the spring and summer of 1887, political groups all over the country began to talk against the high tariff. Not all these groups were Democrats, although relatively few of them were Republican, but from Oregon to Arkansas, and even in the manufacturing states of Pennsylvania and Connecticut, the people began to show their restlessness.

Still, the tariff was an extremely complicated matter, if for no other reason than that each section of the country produced different goods and felt different needs. The Oregon sheep rancher wanted a high tariff on imported wool, to protect his own sales to American manufacturers. But he detested the high tax on sugar, and coffee, and other necessities. The Pennsylvania steel manufacturer cared nothing about the tariff on wool, but he would do all in his power to prevent Congress from cutting the tariff on steel and iron, so foreign manufacturers could sell goods in the United States, and he would have to cut his own prices to meet those of the foreigners, or lose customers.

Everybody wanted some taxes reduced, but not those which affected his business. It was proposed, by some, that the President ask Congress to cut down the taxes on tobacco and liquor in order to reduce the federal surplus of money. The southern states, which produce most of the tobacco and liquor of the nation, were very favorable to this idea; the northern and western states were opposed. Some politicians thought the tariffs on luxury items, such as silk, Chinese cabinets, Indian filigree, and other beautiful playthings of the rich, should be reduced.

President Cleveland said he would not support such a change; what the nation needed, he was certain, was a fair reduction of tariffs, which would help the workingman, and not the very rich. He had talked about tariff reduction from time to time, but in the fall of 1887 he decided he would devote his entire message on the state of the nation to the problems of the surplus and the tariff.

When the President's friends learned what he intended to do, they tried to persuade him against the course. The Republican party stood for high tariffs, and nearly all the most powerful groups in the nation wanted the tariffs on their goods kept high. It was quite all right to talk about tariff inequalities, and to favor a reduction in tariffs, but it was dangerous to be specific.

Cleveland could not be persuaded to ignore the tariff issue or to be quiet about the proposed changes which must be made.

In 1887 the United States had an even greater surplus than in 1886. If the surplus continued to rise the country would be thrown into depression if for no other reason than because of a serious shortage of money. So in December,

1887, President Cleveland demanded that Congress reduce tariffs on necessities. He talked specifically about the need for protecting the jobs of the working man while this was done, but he spoke also of the huge trusts in which manufacturers of the same kinds of products agreed to sell at the same prices, and split up territories among themselves.

Immediately, James G. Blaine replied from Paris. He said that if he were President he would maintain the high tariff and cut the tobacco taxes. As so many Republicans were to claim afterward, Blaine said that through the high tariff, foreigners contributed to our revenue—as bland a misstatement of the facts as could be made, since Americans, not foreigners, paid the ultimate taxes on the foreign goods through high prices.

The tariff issue divided the country into two camps almost immediately, and as in 1884, when the issue was corruption in government, both Republicans and Democrats crossed party lines. That fact alone was a serious threat to President Cleveland's chances for reelection, because in 1888 the Democratic party was smaller and weaker than the Republican party and Democratic victory could be assured only if Cleveland could win Republican votes and independent votes without losing any important part of the Democratic vote.

In April, the House of Representatives Committee on Ways and Means considered the President's tariff proposal, a bill which would reduce the tariff by $53,000,000 and other taxes by about $24,000,000, wiping out most of the surplus expected that year. The debate in Congress continued for three months, the Republicans lining up for the high tariff as it stood, and the Democrats, generally speaking, taking the President's side that the tariff should be revised. Finally, the President won his battle for the tariff, but at the cost of unity in his own party and the arousal of the Republicans. He had given them an issue on which they

could pull together, and about which they could talk endlessly.

Early in June the Democrats held their national convention in St. Louis. President Cleveland was renominated
easily, although the leaders of Tammany Hall were opposed
to him again. Two weeks later the Republicans met in
Chicago, many of them expecting to nominate James G.
Blaine once again, but Blaine remained in Europe and as
the convention met he cabled the Republicans that he
would not accept the nomination if it came to him. The
only other strong candidate who was well known was John
Sherman of Ohio, an old and respected senator, who was
also the brother of General Sherman. Finally, however, the
Republicans nominated Benjamin Harrison of Indiana, a
simple little man who had few attributes of greatness, but
few faults from the political point of view. He was amiable
and quiet, and in the campaign against Cleveland the issue
would not be Harrison's abilities but Grover Cleveland's
record in the Presidency.

The political campaign of 1888 was intensely personal
as had been the campaign of 1884. The President's personal
life was again an issue—this time the rumor-spreaders said
that he beat his young wife and mistreated everyone around
him. The obvious issue of the campaign was the tariff, and
it helped the Republicans significantly because many
wealthy merchants and industrialists contributed heavily
to the Republican campaign.

Andrew Carnegie supported the Republicans with contributions, and so did John Wanamaker, the merchant, who
was finance chairman of the Republican party that year.
Wanamaker raised $100,000 in a few hours from ten
wealthy businessmen in Philadelphia.

From the beginning the Republicans set out to create
what Chauncey Depew, the President of the New York Central Railroad, called a "cyclone of fear" that jobs and wealth

would disappear if the Democrats won and the tariff was reduced.

President Cleveland did not campaign since he believed it beneath the dignity of the Presidency. Benjamin Harrison worked hard—he made ninety-four major speeches during his campaign, most of them directed against the President's tariff policy. Some manufacturers said they would have to close their plants if the Democrats won and the tariff on raw materials used in manufacturing their products was lowered. What they meant, of course, was that they would have to lower their prices or suffer in competition with foreign manufacturers, but they did not admit to this belief, and they convinced many officials of organized labor and many workingmen that high tariffs helped keep jobs stable and wages steady.

The tariff was important, and yet it played only one part in the election campaign. There were many other issues and schemes which were to be equally important. New York, the largest state in population, leaned heavily to the Republicans because Tammany Hall had so little use for President Cleveland that the Tammany chiefs did almost nothing to help him.

In 1884 a minor incident had helped Cleveland win the Presidency—when the Catholics of the crowded eastern cities were aroused by the cry of Rum, Romanism, and Rebellion. In 1888 an equally minor incident occurred to hurt Cleveland, largely because it could be connected to the tariff issue. From the beginning of the year James G. Blaine, in Europe, had been saying that the British regarded President Cleveland's low tariff policy as an opening for free trade, and to many Americans this indicated that the American market would be deluged with British manufactured products which would force the closing of factories and throw thousands of men out of work. The tariff was as much an emotional issue as an economic problem, and it was tied up with anti-British sentiment which remained as a leftover from the Revolution and the War of 1812, nurtured by a number of incidents involving American ships and American interests in Latin America, and even by a long-standing dispute over fishing rights with Canada. The Canadian dispute came up again that summer and feeling against the British continued to be strong. Whenever anti-British sentiment could be brought into the campaign the Republicans could count on some extra votes, if they pasted the label of pro-British on President Cleveland.

Halfway through the campaign, in September, Sir Lionel Sackville-West, the British minister in Washington, received a letter from a man who called himself Charles F. Murchison. Murchison said he was English-born, although he had since become a citizen of the United States, and he had a soft spot in his heart for England. If he wanted to help out his old homeland, Murchison asked, how should he vote in the coming election?

Sir Lionel allowed himself to be caught in the trap. He replied to Mr. Murchison that the Democratic party certainly seemed to be friendly to England.

In reality, there was no Mr. Murchison. The letter had been written to Sir Lionel by a Republican politician, and when he received the revealing answer, he took it to Republican headquarters, where it was released to the press.

President Cleveland was shocked, and told Secretary of State Bayard to demand that the British government call Sir Lionel home since he had interfered in an American election. The British did not call him home, and Cleveland had him sent home. The damage was done, nevertheless, and thousands of American citizens voted for the Republican candidate not so much because they were for

Harrison or against Cleveland, but because they were against Great Britain and resented what they thought was interference in the American system of government.

Throughout the election campaign, Cleveland kept his dignity. Personally, he did not want to serve another term as President, although he did believe that it would be best for the country if the Democrats were returned to office. Democratic politicians blamed Cleveland for raising the issue of the tariff, and thus dividing the party, uniting the Republicans, and giving them the strength of business support. The President paid no attention to these men, nor was he sorry when at the end of the campaign many of them told him he would be defeated.

"What is the use of being elected or re-elected unless you stand for something?" President Cleveland asked.

On election day the President waited for the results quietly in the White House library, and when he learned that he had been defeated, he said that he regretted nothing, for it was better to be defeated in fighting for a principle than to win if that meant avoiding the issue he felt was all-important. He was certain that the tariff reform was still needed to save the economy of the country and that no matter what the Republicans did in the next few years, the tariff would be lowered. With a light heart, Grover Cleveland prepared to leave the White House and Washington to take up life as a private citizen once more.

☆ victory again

How does a President of the United States feel when he has been defeated in his campaign for re-election and must leave the White House? Grover Cleveland never felt better, for he was thoroughly reconciled to the idea of becoming a private citizen. His greatest personal problem, as the Presidential term neared its end, was to decide where to live and what to do with himself.

He had been asked about returning to Buffalo, but Cleveland would not think of it. Of all the cities in the United States, Buffalo was the one he would never live in, for Buffalo had begun the rumors, in two elections, about Cleveland's private life which gave him so much pain, and many of the rumor-mongers and gossips were people Cleveland had known in his years in the city on Lake Erie. Cleveland sputtered angrily when friends spoke to him of Buffalo, even in 1889.

The President was fond of New Jersey, where he had been born and where he lived during his earliest years, but he was asked to go to many other states, either to practice law or to engage in business. He would not remain in Washington, both he and Mrs. Cleveland were certain of that much, for with a Republican administration coming in, the atmosphere in Washington would change, and he expected to be uncomfortable if he stayed on in the capital.

There is a story that when Mrs. Cleveland was packing
their belongings and making ready to turn the White
House over to the new President and his family, she
warned the servant to take good care of the furniture because she and Mr. Cleveland would be coming back in
four years. Grover Cleveland had no such thoughts, nor
did he seem to have any desire to return to Washington.
He sold the Georgetown Heights house he had purchased
—Oak View—for a profit of $100,000. That profit solved
any financial problems which might have arisen in the
years since he had left Buffalo. Cleveland had amassed
a fairly large fortune when he practiced law in Buffalo,
but the years in public office, as mayor, governor, and
President, had eaten deeply into his funds, since in those
days Americans did not believe in paying public officials
as much as was really required to do the job. Particularly
as President, even though the Clevelands lived quietly, he
was underpaid; and he had spent much of his $50,000 a
year on official entertainments, as demanded of the President of the United States.

Since he was relieved of responsibility, Cleveland felt
absolutely free to speak his mind about national problems.
He had always been forthright when forced to make a
decision between what was right and moral in government
and what was wrong, even if it did not seem to be politically wise, but not always had Cleveland been in a position
to consider the philosophy of government. Now he did
think that way, and talked of the growing problems of the
nation, because the rich were growing richer and the poor
were growing poorer, and the farmers were falling into
debt. Later, in the years after his death, some historians
characterized Cleveland as the last American President of
the purely business mold, and yet Cleveland was not a
businessman in any way, nor did he hold any particular

love for business. Looking around him in the last months of his first term, Cleveland saw that the gulf between employers and workers was growing wide, and that two classes of society were being formed—one made up of the very rich, and the other class made up of the very poor. He also saw that corporations, instead of becoming the salvation of the public, were becoming the masters, and that a handful of rich men were seizing control of American industry through holding companies and trusts.

The last few months of Cleveland's first term were as exciting as any period in history since the Civil War. Following his demand that Lord Sackville-West return to England, the British Foreign Office decided to teach the stripling American government a lesson and failed to send another minister to Washington. That made the position of the American minister in London laughable. He resented the constant insult to his country, and he asked Secretary of State Bayard to let him come home. The Secretary of State was a cautious man who did not want trouble, particularly in these last few months, but the minister appealed to Cleveland, who told him to pack his bags and leave London. For the first time since the Sackville-West affair, American-British relations were again on an equal footing.

Few Americans know how close Cleveland brought the United States to war with Germany in 1889. Had it not been for an Act of God, perhaps war would have come— at least President Cleveland was prepared for it and would have accepted war as necessary to uphold his position on a matter of principle.

This period of history marked the most extensive German effort to acquire an empire in the far reaches of the world. Chancellor Bismarck expanded German influence in China, in Africa, and in the islands dotting the Pacific ocean which were, in those days of coal burning ships, important as naval bases and refueling stations.

For many years the United States, Britain, and Germany had maintained trade relations and bases in Samoa, but the Germans were the most aggressive of all, and in 1888 German residents exiled King Malietoa and put their own man in his place. The next step would be to give favored treatment to the Germans, and eventually to force the Americans and British out altogether.

Cleveland was angry and sent a message to Congress in January, in which he explained his efforts to protect American interests in Samoa. He also dispatched several American warships to Apia, the capital of Samoa, in case they were needed for action.

A few weeks later, Cleveland was barely dissuaded from sending another message on Samoa to Congress. He had prepared the message and was ready to send it—but if he had sent it, quite probably it would have brought war. He said—privately as it turned out—that the Germans were trying to subvert the government of Samoa for their own purposes.

Even after Cleveland was persuaded to be calm, the situation continued to be tense. American officers in Samoa were annoyed with the Germans. The Germans increased their naval strength in Apia harbor. There seemed to be every reason to believe war would begin any day, as Cleveland's term ended and President Harrison took office. But as the two naval forces lay in the harbor at Apia waiting for some misstep by the other or some word from home, a hurricane—typhoon they called them in Pacific waters—moved in on Apia. Within a few hours all the ships in the harbor were sunk, their bellies torn open on the sharp coral reefs which surrounded the deep waters—all but the British cruiser *Calliope*, which miraculously escaped. For years afterwards visitors could see the rusting skeletons of the ships which had nearly gone to war, especially the mighty *Adler,* one of Bismarck's prides.

Among the important official business of Cleveland's last days was the appointment of Melville W. Fuller as Chief Justice of the Supreme Court, an appointment which was to have a lasting effect on the American government. Fuller was an extremely conservative judge who believed nothing should infringe on the rights of the individual to hold and enjoy property. He was what is called a strict constructionist, in regard to the United States Constitution, and refused to reinterpret the Constitution to cover new situations as they arose. Consequently, while many men in government, including President Cleveland, were cognizant of the need to regulate corporations and the growing power of the trusts, the Supreme Court resisted those changes for many years. It was not until Fuller died in 1910 that the character of the court was liberalized. This appointment made by President Cleveland in 1888 was to affect the destiny of the United States for twenty-two years.

Once Benjamin Harrison was sworn in on March 4, 1889, Grover Cleveland and his wife moved to New York. They had decided on New York because a prominent law firm had asked Cleveland to share their office space (although he never became a partner in that firm). Cleveland also looked kindly on New York City as a place in which to live and practice law because he had many friends in the city, and he had already been accepted by the bar of New York State, years ago, so there were no technical difficulties about resuming private law practice.

At first the Clevelands moved into a house at 816 Madison Avenue, near 68th Street, then a fashionable residential district. They lived in a narrow four story house of the style so typical in New York, and Cleveland rode the elevated trains each day down to his office not far from Wall Street. He spent most of his working hours at the office, gladly greeting business and personal friends, and lunching either at a club or at a restaurant with a friend. He was not inclined to attend parties and he entertained very little at home.

In the summer, Cleveland liked to go hunting and fishing, particularly fishing, and at this stage of life he was persuaded there was no better fishing and vacation spot than the Sippican Harbor area of Massachusetts. Cleveland and his wife spent many summers there, starting in 1888, and it was not long after his retirement to private life that he bought a cottage and a number of acres of land at a place called Buzzards Bay. He named the cottage Gray Gables. When he visited the spot, day after day he went fishing, in a small boat just off the shore, or further out in a good-sized sloop owned by a local fishing captain who usually managed to find the bluefish, rock bass, and tautogs which delighted Cleveland's heart and eye.

For a year Cleveland refused to be drawn into politics at all, then his first political speech, made in Boston, dealt with the need for election reforms. A year later he was showing far more interest in politics. After the McKinley tariff law had begun to arouse people all over the country against the raised tariffs and the issue of silver coinage was becoming an important political matter, Cleveland wanted the nomination as President again.

In 1889, when the Republican administration came into power it found itself faced with issues as explosive as Samoa, but without Acts of God to avert disaster or to make small disaster serve a greater end, as had the sinking of the German and American fleet in Apia harbor. It was apparent, even had not Cleveland called it to public attention, that the trusts were sucking out the blood of American initiative and converting the nation into a series of feudal landholds. The Republican Congress had to face this issue, whether it liked to control the trusts (most of them Republican in alignment) or would rather leave them alone. One of the most important pieces of legislation in Benjamin Harrison's administration was the Sherman Anti-Trust law, and if we now wonder why it seems so obscure and so indefinite in its provisions about trusts, the reason is clear in the distaste of the Congressmen for any kind of action at all. They passed to the courts the responsibility for definition of trusts and the offenses under the law, and the courts were to struggle with those thereafter, creating, by necessity, a kind of legislation by the judiciary.

By the spring of 1890 the Republicans had changed the tariff law—but in changing it they had not really lowered tariffs at all. The new law was drawn by William McKinley in the House of Representatives. Congress was slow in making the change, and after the new tariff rates had been published, it was five months before the new rates became law. In those five months traders put in stocks of goods bought at the old rates. Then, after the law had passed and the tariff on some goods had gone up, the traders who had bought those goods raised the prices, creating huge profits for themselves, and even greater stocks of resentment among the voters. In the Congressional elections of 1890 the Republicans carried only eighty-eight seats in the House of Representatives, of a total of three hundred and thirty-two. It was the worst defeat the Republican party had ever suffered since the party's beginnings in 1856.

The tariff was one important issue, an issue on which Cleveland had chosen to stand or fall in 1888. Two years later his position was vindicated, but at the same time another issue was already overpowering the tariff, the issue of silver coinage.

During the first Cleveland administration the men in Congress who came from the mining states of the west and the men from the farm states of the middle west and south combined to press for an increase in the amount of silver money in circulation. The mining men wanted more silver, of course, because that gave them a good market for their ore. The farmers and others whose way of life meant they were likely to be in debt, for advances against crops, or for mortgages on property—all these groups wanted an increase in silver coinage. They wanted money to become more plentiful, knowing that its value in relation to property would decrease; but a farmer who had borrowed $10,000 to buy a piece of land could only be better off if the land value suddenly went to $20,000, even when this was caused by the money becoming less valuable. The farmer did not stop to consider whether or not other increases in prices, such as food and clothing and farm supplies, might not more than wipe out the increase he thought he was receiving in his capital through the cheapening of the currency. This could only be demonstrated in fact, and even then some people were better off in inflation times and some were not.

Cleveland took the position that the nation as a whole was much worse off in times of inflation, and he proposed to keep the national economy stable. When the Republicans came to power in 1888 they had neatly sidestepped the issue. They had passed a silver bill which forced the treasury to purchase 4,500,000 ounces of silver every month, but the government bought this money with treasury notes which were redeemable in gold or silver coin, whichever the government wanted to give. This bill did not satisfy the advocates of free silver—who wanted the government to buy every ounce of silver the miners produced and turn it into money. Nor did it satisfy the "sound money" men, who wanted to control the amount of silver in circulation and keep silver as a subsidiary metal, used largely for small coins. Still, while the new law did not satisfy either side, it kept the struggle from breaking out immediately and hurting the Republican Congress. This bill, also submitted by Senator Sherman, was called the Sherman Silver Purchase Act.

As the issue was being debated in Congress, Cleveland was asked for an opinion and he came out flatly against free silver. His enemies, in Tammany and elsewhere, could not have been more pleased, for they felt sure this would disqualify the former President before the nominating convention of 1892. Cleveland's principal opponent for the nomination was David B. Hill, the machine politician and friend of Tammany, who had been Cleveland's lieutenant governor in New York and had then gone on to become governor and to be elected to the United States Senate. Hill had sought election to the Senate in 1891, largely because he hoped to be able to influence Democrats in Congress into giving him the Presidential nomination in 1892.

Hill tried to win the nomination, and his friends tried to help him, by using the lowest of tricks. When the date of the national convention was announced in January, 1892, the Hill supporters, who controlled the state Democratic committee, called a convention for February. They did this for a very simple reason: by holding the state convention in February they could make sure that most of the farmers and Democrats from little towns around New York would not be able to attend, and the political bosses from New York, Albany, Buffalo, and the other cities could be sure of controlling the convention. It worked just as they had expected; the roads from the small towns were blocked by snow and the farmers could not leave their homes unattended, so the political bosses won the day, and the convention delegates were theirs, to support David B. Hill.

The Hill boom did not work out, however. By pushing for their candidate so early in the year, the Democratic bosses made him a target, and as the weeks rolled by, Democrats around the rest of the country began to realize that the Hill victory in New York had been dishonest and manufactured. Instead of pushing Cleveland out of the political scene, the action of the political bosses had created sympathy for him.

When the Democratic National Convention met at the end of June, Cleveland was nominated on the first ballot. He was so confident and casual that while the balloting was in progress he was at his cottage drying his fishing lines. In many ways, the former President was a changed man. No longer did he spend sixteen or eighteen hours a day at his desk. His first child, Ruth, had been born in October, 1891, and now, in the summer of 1892, he loved to go driving, perhaps down to the post office in the village near Gray Gables, to show off his daughter and his wife to the villagers. He had become more mellow, and yet he retained the same stiffness of character when it came to matters of good government and policies he believed in.

If Cleveland had seemed lackadaisical in the campaign of 1888, and if he had seemed only mildly interested in securing the nomination in 1892, all signs of indecision vanished once he was nominated. He remained at Gray Gables during most of the summer of 1892, but spent very little time fishing or enjoying himself. Most of his waking hours were spent attending to correspondence, urging

Democratic leaders all across the country to work harder
than ever before to get out the vote and win a victory for
Cleveland and the party.

One of Cleveland's most serious problems was the antagonism of the Hill followers in New York State, and the
failure of Tammany Hall to get out and work for a Cleveland victory. William Whitney, Cleveland's former Secretary of the Navy, pleaded with the big candidate to make
his peace with Tammany, but Cleveland could be very
stubborn when he wanted to be, and although he understood as well as anyone how important New York State
was to victory, he would do nothing to make friends.

Finally, Whitney did persuade Cleveland at least to
come to New York City and talk with the Tammany bosses
—Sheehan (his old enemy from Buffalo), Edward Murphy,
Jr., and Richard Croker. Cleveland reluctantly hauled his
huge bulk onto a train and came to the city to stay at his
favorite Victoria Hotel, where he would meet the Tammany men.

William Whitney tried to smooth the occasion by making it a dinner meeting and giving all these rough-tem-
pered men the best dinner money could afford. During
the dinner the conversation was friendly enough, on every
topic other than politics, which went unmentioned. Then,
over cigars, the dinner dishes cleared away, they got down
to business.

Cleveland asked how the campaign was going.

Not very well, said the Tammany men, and Sheehan
began to explain the reason for it.

He and his friends were embittered because Cleveland's
Independent Republican followers and others were attacking Tammany as crooked and dishonest. As long as this
continued, they would not put Tammany squarely behind the candidate—they could not even if they wanted to,

because the Tammany men resented the attacks and would not work under the circumstances.

Further, the Tammany chiefs said, they wanted promises from Cleveland that if he were elected he would give Tammany the patronage it wanted for New York City. They recalled that in 1885 Cleveland had given them nothing.

Cleveland smacked his hand on the table and shouted that he would promise nothing. When they continued to press him, he said he would resign his candidacy if they continued to press, and (some reports have it) he also threatened to tell the people of the nation exactly why he was resigning.

Whatever the truth of that story, it was apparent at the end of the meeting that Cleveland had his way. Tammany agreed to work for him, without any specific promises, and a few days later even Hill announced he was for Cleveland.

Once the problem within the Democratic party was solved every effort was put to winning the election. Surprisingly enough, in view of past political campaigns, the election campaign of 1892 was the most sedate and reasoned since the end of the Civil War. There were no complaints about Cleveland's morals, and no harassments by either side. Even the issue of the Civil War was left at rest for the first time. Harrison's followers admitted that Cleveland would make an honest President and Cleveland's men paid Harrison the same tribute. The fireworks, such as they happened to be, were almost entirely in the hands of the Populist party, which had emerged from a number of groups of dissatisfied debtors and workers and farmers to nominate James B. Weaver for the Presidency. The Populists were a real threat in the west and south, but their strength was somewhat over-emphasized because

Democrats in the west (who did not hope to win) threw their votes to Populist candidates to keep the Republicans from winning, and Republicans in the south, who knew they would lose, also threw votes to the Populists to keep southern Democrats from victory.

In spite of this peculiar political trading, Cleveland won a resounding victory, the strongest victory of any political candidate since Lincoln's victory in the election of 1864, and with the victory, the awful responsibility of leading the nation again for four long years.

☆ depression

BETWEEN ELECTION DAY and his inauguration in March, 1893, Grover Cleveland was hopeful, and even elated a good part of the time, as he looked forward to reassuming responsibility and the exercise of his political judgments. Personally, Cleveland would rather have stayed in private life, fishing in the summers, and practicing law in the winter, but having decided that he was needed in government once again he had put aside personal considerations at the time he accepted the nomination and had once again devoted himself to politics and statesmanship. There was, moreover, the constant lure of the Presidency before him, for no man, once he has tasted political power, finds it easy to give it up until he has exhausted his legal and moral rights to the retention of power. General Grant, for example, would not have been averse to accepting a third term as President of the United States, if he had been sufficiently urged by his Republican contemporaries.

It would be foolish to say that Cleveland was not prepared to enjoy his high office during the second term, but he entered the Presidency for the second time fully cognizant of the demands of the office and the responsibilities which he had undertaken.

Once his cabinet was appointed, Cleveland again had to withstand a long and constant stream of office-seekers and political leaders who wanted offices for others. William Jennings Bryan, a relatively obscure member of Congress from Nebraska, was one of these politicians who sought favors for others. He wanted control of a number of postmasterships in Nebraska. Bryan did not get all he wanted, however, although Cleveland did try in the interest of party unity to give the politicians some of the patronage they requested. This yielding to party pressure made Cleveland less popular with the reformers, and yet he did not yield enough to suit the Democrats. Perhaps the best assessment of his course lies in his association with Theodore Roosevelt, with whom Cleveland had associated during his short term as governor of New York—when Roosevelt was Republican leader in the Assembly.

Under the Harrison administration, Roosevelt had been chosen as a Civil Service commissioner. When Cleveland was re-elected, it was generally thought that Roosevelt would be asked to resign, but Cleveland knew Roosevelt, was certain of his ability and honesty, and kept him on in the job. Roosevelt felt no particular loyalty to Cleveland for this, and was quick to criticize the Democratic administration—but he did report shortly after the inauguration that on balance he found the administration better than both the first Cleveland administration and the Harrison administration. It was quite an admission for the young Republican, who had been so partisan in the election of 1884 that while he hated the spoils system and corruption he had felt forced to support James G. Blaine for the Presidency instead of following his emotions and joining the Mugwumps.

In the four years to come, Cleveland was to show that he had not given up his belief in sound and honest government, or in the value of the merit system. He was to add 44,000 jobs to the Civil Service system, bringing that system to a total of 86,000 jobs, and under the Cleveland administration the careless operation of the post office, which had been run like a department store by John Wanamaker, was completely reversed.

As Cleveland stepped into office in 1893, however, he faced problems which made the Civil Service question and job-hunting by Democratic politicians seem relatively unimportant. The Sherman Silver Purchase Act had been in effect just a little more than two years, but in that short time the federal government had lost almost all of the tremendous gold reserve of the first Cleveland administration. During Cleveland's first term in office he had been plagued by the accumulation of too much money in the hands of the treasury. In his second administration he was immediately faced with the prospect of not enough good money—gold—in the treasury. The Gold Reserve, set by the Congress at $100,000,000, had fallen to less than a million dollars above that limit. If it fell below a hundred million dollars—which could happen in a matter of days— the federal government's credit would be hurt, and that meant the economy of the whole country would be in danger.

The Secretary of the Treasury, John Griffin Carlisle, immediately tried to persuade the banks to give gold to the treasury, in exchange for paper money. The banks did turn over $25,000,000 to the treasury in those first few weeks, but the flood of paper money descending on the treasury did not end. There was a simple reason for this flow.

When Senator Sherman had presented his Silver Purchase Act, it stated that the treasury could pay out metal money against paper money, either in gold or silver, as it preferred. If half the people wanted gold and the other half wanted silver, there should have been very little problem. But the fact was that gold and silver were not interchangeable, and everyone in the country knew that, even the miners. When people appeared at the treasury to change their paper money into metal money, practically no one asked for silver; almost everyone asked for gold. The government could have paid silver anyhow, but this would have undermined the confidence of the people in the paper money. Men who had originally changed gold into paper with the understanding that they could change it back any time they wanted to would not be inclined to trust the government again, and instead of using paper money they would hoard their gold, hard as it might be to transport.

The proof of the basic dishonesty in the Free Silver Bloc's philosophy lay in the actions of the mining men themselves. They mined silver and gold together usually (far more silver than gold lies in a vein) and they sold their silver, under the Silver Purchase Act, to a treasury which was bound to buy the silver at the rate of 4,500,000 ounces every month. Even this amount did not satisfy the miners, who were mining more ore than that and agitating for the government to buy every ounce of it. When the government did buy silver, it paid the mining men in paper money that could be redeemed in either gold or silver; but when the miners redeemed the paper money, they took gold, not silver. Consequently the silver began to stack up in the treasury and the gold flowed out dangerously fast. There was nothing the federal government could do with its silver supply—no other country wanted silver; every one in every country recognized the superior value of gold. All the federal government could do was keep taking in silver and keep paying out gold. If Cleveland had allowed the treasury to start paying out silver instead of gold the panic would have been immediate and disastrous.

Yet Cleveland's promise, in April, that the government would pay out only gold did not save the country from depression. Bankers and investors knew what was happening. They could see that the treasury was being milked, and, fearing that they would be caught short, the investors began to turn in their paper money, take gold, and hoard it.

Late in February, before Cleveland's inauguration, the loss of gold to the treasury had seemed severe enough. Gold had been leaving the country rapidly, at the rate of fifty million dollars in 1892. The banking firms of the nation appealed to Cleveland to call a special session of Congress after March 4, when Congress would adjourn once the new administration was inaugurated. The bankers wanted the Sherman Silver Purchase Act repealed.

Cleveland thought the matter over, but in the end he refused to take such rapid action. He wanted to be sure the people of the country realized it was the silver act which had put the country into depression.

Before the end of February, the nation was shocked to wake up one morning and discover that the Philadelphia and Reading Railroad had gone bankrupt, owing $125 million. The Reading failure was followed by others, some financial houses began to collapse, and on May 5 the National Cordage Company went into bankruptcy.

The only importance of National Cordage lay in its reputation: the company had gained a great deal of notoriety as a fast-moving operation by slick financiers, and in April it had decided on a large cash dividend to be paid in May. The stock of the company, valued at one hundred and forty-seven in January, fell to ten. The market dropped, and investors tried to liquidate their holdings for whatever the market would bring.

One problem, which would plague the nation for another forty years, was the collapse of the banking system.

It was the practice of small town banks to keep their cash on deposit with city banks at two percent interest. The city banks needed the money; the country banks always had more money in hand than they needed except in emergency, and it was altogether an admirable way for the small banks to pick up a little extra income. But when the crisis came, the farmers and small town folk insisted on having their savings; many small town banks did not have the cash on hand and suspended payments until the cash arrived—which meant they failed, for no citizen would again put money in that bank.

The reformers, in particular, wanted President Cleveland to call a special session of Congress to deal with the currency question, and as time went on and the business world found itself unable to extricate itself from the mess it had created, Cleveland found himself leaning toward that course.

Monetary problems, however, were not the only matters which demanded his attention. Nor was he certain that until the public demanded the repeal of the Silver Purchase Act he could force the repeal through Congress, no matter how great his personal prestige.

He was also disturbed by the continual claims of office-seekers on his time, and the knotty problem of imperialism, which had again raised its head in Hawaii.

For a number of years Americans had been moving into Hawaii in increasing numbers, exploiting the island kingdom's cheap labor and rich natural resources to create huge land empires, fortunes, and vested interests. Pineapple and sugar plantations, shipping empires and trading fortunes grew larger and larger, as Hawaii's trade with the mainland increased.

Long before, in 1851, King Kamehameha had given the American Commissioner in Honolulu a deed to the Hawaiian Islands, ceding sovereignty to the United States.

The king had done this because the French imperialists, at that moment, were trying to move in and make Hawaii a French colony. Daniel Webster was the American Secretary of State that year and refused the gift, although he warned France off and told the world that the United States Navy would protect the sovereignty of Hawaii. It was easy enough to see how American traders received concessions, then, from a grateful Hawaiian government. By 1887 King Kalahua had been forced to declare a constitutional monarchy, forced in reality by the American guests who had been invited to make their fortunes in the land. During Cleveland's first term of office, the relations between the United States and Hawaii had been correct and friendly. While American business was dominant there, Cleveland would countenance no talk about annexation and spoke of the necessity of preserving Hawaiian independence.

After Cleveland left office in 1889 the American minister to Hawaii, John Stevens, began to work for American annexation of Hawaii. James G. Blaine was Secretary of State; he had no particular antipathy to imperialism; and he did nothing to stop Stevens in his scheming.

In 1891, King Kalahua died and his sister Princess Liliuokalani ascended the throne. The new queen had some very decided ambitions of her own: she hated the missionaries and the rich whites who had reaped fortunes in the land and now lorded it over her people. She detested the constitution, which hindered her in taking revenge on her enemies and curbed her power over her subjects and the riches of the islands. She decided that she would overthrow the constitution, take the vote away from the whites (who had been made citizens by the constitution), and establish her own absolute rule. Minister Stevens and the Americans lost no time in taking action when they heard that she intended to do this in January, 1893.

Minister Stevens was concerned, but the white community, led by Lorrin A. Thurston, Henry Waterhouse, and
Sanford F. Dole, was seriously worried, for neither life nor
property would be safe if Liliuokalani had her way. She
was perfectly prepared to wipe out the white community
and put the merchants' heads beneath the executioner's ax.

The whites formed a committee of public safety, but for
a time they were in serious trouble. Minister Stevens was
not in Honolulu when the revolution broke. He was on a
cruise to Hilo aboard the U. S. warship *Boston,* which carried a detachment of United States marines. The white
population of Honolulu wanted to force the issue against
the Queen, but they could raise only eighty fighting men,
and the Royal Army consisted of five hundred men, four
or five cannons, and twenty policemen. The eighty whites
could not stand against them.

Fortunately for the revolutionaries, Minister Stevens
and the *Boston* returned to Honolulu before any flareup
had occurred. The Americans asked him to land marines
and he did so. Three days later the monarchy was outlawed and Stevens, representing the United States, had
recognized the Provisional Government. President Dole
raised the American flag over the government buildings
and spoke of his government as a "protectorate" which
would last until the United States Congress annexed
Hawaii.

The Provisional Government then sent off five commissioners to ask President Harrison to annex the islands.
Harrison sent a treaty to the Senate, providing for annexation, and the treaty was resting there when Cleveland was
inaugurated. No one knew how Cleveland felt about the
annexation, because he flatly refused to discuss government policies of the previous administration between election day and his own resumption of responsibility.

Within a week after his inauguration, Cleveland sent a

five line note to the Senate, withdrawing the treaty for
further study. He wanted to find out what this annexation
proposal meant, and whose idea it really was. When he
saw the treaty he became suspicious, for there were names
on the treaty, but not a Polynesian name among them, nor
was he certain that the United States government had not
played a part in the overthrow of Queen Liliuokalani's
monarchy. Besides, before his inauguration he had received a letter from Liliuokalani in which she expressed
her grievance and asked him to listen to the case presented
by her agent in Washington. Cleveland was willing to
listen; further, he was willing to send a representative of
his own to Hawaii to try to get the facts, and he insisted
on doing this before going any further with the treaty.
He did not tell his representative how he felt about the
Hawaiian question. He simply asked for information.
Then, he sat down to wait until he received the information before taking another step relative to Hawaii, showing a sense of responsibility and a patience he had not
indicated in foreign affairs in his previous administration.
Time and experience, obviously, had made Cleveland a
more competent President in 1893 than he had been in
1885. Time was to test him almost beyond endurance in
the next four years, for although the period of 1893 to
1897 is not widely recognized as an era of activity in American history, these were the days of some of the most fla-
grant violence, abuse of law, and social upheaval in the history of the American nation. It would take a strong President at the helm in the four years ahead to guide a dis-
united and aroused nation; it was fortunate that the voters
had chosen just such a man.

✫ cancer!

ONE DAY IN APRIL, 1893, the federal gold reserve fell to $97,000,000, three million dollars below the limit set by Congress beyond which the gold reserve must never be allowed to fall. The President began to receive hundreds of letters from citizens who proposed various solutions to the problem of gold and silver, letters from eccentrics and professional busybodies; but also letters from such men as Henry Clews, the financier, August Belmont, the banker, and Andrew Carnegie, the steel manufacturer.

One financial house noted in the spring that the actual value of the silver dollar on the world market had fallen to an equivalent of fifty-three cents—while the gold dollar had kept its value at one hundred cents. All this was attributed to the flood of silver which had come into world markets—not just the American market but the Indian market and the European market as well. Silver was becoming less valuable every day as more and more of it was poured out of the mines into the treasuries of the nations of the world. By forcing the American government to buy silver as though it were worth a hundred cents on the dollar, the Sherman law was driving the United States toward bankruptcy.

By the first of June, 1893, nearly everyone in the nation accepted the truth, outside the group of selfish mining men and others who were well served by inflation. On June 4 the President indicated to a newspaperman that he was almost ready to call Congress into special session to demand a change in the law—to stop the silver purchases and put silver back into a subsidiary place as a money metal. Immediately both sides began to prepare themselves for the coming fight. Cleveland had hoped to let the issue rest until the regular session of Congress, but it was impossible. Action must be taken immediately, if the economy was to be stabilized at all.

While the President was pondering the silver question, he developed a sore spot on the roof of his mouth, and on Sunday, June 18, he called in the official government physician, Dr. R. M. O'Reilly, to check it. Dr. O'Reilly examined the rough spot and discovered an ulcer on the roof of the President's mouth, about the size of a quarter of a dollar, extending from the back molars to a point about a third of an inch from the middle line of the mouth. During the examination, the doctor removed a small piece of the diseased tissue and sent it to the Army Medical Museum for analysis. He was careful to say nothing about the name or position of the patient.

The pathologist who examined the issue reported that it was almost certainly cancerous. How long had it been there? Cleveland was not quite sure, but he knew it had not bothered him on inauguration day or before. Since then, he had been so busy one day seemed to melt into the next.

Dr. O'Reilly recommended an operation. Cleveland then called his personal physician down from New York —Dr. Joseph D. Bryant, who had been his doctor and friend for many years. Dr. Bryant confirmed the diagnosis and also recommended an operation.

The President was disturbed, most of all because he had planned to call Congress into session to solve the money question.

"Were it in *my* mouth I would have it removed at once," Dr. Bryant said.

Cleveland agreed to the operation, but since it was so serious a matter, and the country was in such a state of nervousness, he insisted that the operation and the illness be kept completely secret. From the malignant material, it was impossible for the doctors to tell exactly what they would find when they operated, and it was also impossible to know whether or not the cancer would spread. Cleveland was not at all sure he would survive either the operation or the period just after it, when, if the doctors had not managed to remove all the material, his fate might be sealed.

Politically, the President faced a number of serious problems. If he died without saying anything about the Sherman Silver Purchase law, it was doubtful if anything would be done. Adlai Stevenson, his Vice-President, had been selected as a favor to the western states, and Stevenson was an advocate of silver. He could not be expected to press the issue.

Cleveland learned from his doctors that it would take about five weeks for the operation and recuperation, and he made his plans accordingly. On June 30, he released a call to Congress, asking for a special session to begin August 7. On that same day the President left the White House for New York City. He told everyone he was going to take a cruise on Commodore E. C. Benedict's yacht, the *Oneida*, and would eventually arrive at Gray Gables, where Mrs. Cleveland and their daughter had already gone to escape the Washington summer heat.

The President took the 4:20 train from the Union Station for New York. Literally, he slipped out of the city before anyone but his intimates knew he was gone, to ride a car of the Pennsylvania Railroad on the journey whose end he could not foresee.

Cleveland knew the operation was to be serious—in those days any operation was serious, and further, Cleveland's physical condition gave some cause for concern, for although he was robust, he was fifty-six years old, and greatly overweight for any age.

Earlier that day the doctors met at the Battery, on the lower tip of Manhattan island, and were rowed out to the yacht which lay a considerable distance out in the harbor. On the *Oneida,* they converted the living room into an operating room, disinfected the ship, set up the operating equipment, and checked to be sure that all the instruments, dressings, and drugs they might need had been placed on board. Four doctors and a dentist were present, to be joined by Dr. Bryant, who had come up from Washington with Daniel Lamont, Secretary of War and Cleveland's intimate friend and private secretary during the first administration. The doctors and the dentist would exert every effort to save the President's life, and Secretary Lamont would do everything he could to save the President's secret, unless the worst came.

Cleveland's party arrived in the middle of the evening and was immediately taken to the yacht. He lighted a cigar and sat on deck until near midnight, talking to Commodore Benedict. Then he went to bed, and despite the coming ordeal, slept soundly the whole night through.

On the following morning, July 1, the surgeons gave him a careful physical examination while he was still in bed. They were concerned because he was obviously near physical exhaustion after four months of constant crisis and the nagging of the office-seekers who preyed on Cleveland's mind and conscience without end. Yet he was well enough for the operation, they decided, and the difficult job could begin.

The doctors came to the ship that morning and Commodore Benedict ordered the crew to hoist the anchor and get the yacht under way, since the President wanted to be sure no newspapermen discovered what was happening aboard the *Oneida* on that day. The doctors left the deck and moved below into the cabinet; some of them might be recognized by their friends if they stayed on deck, and the ship was headed at half speed up the East River, where they would soon pass Bellevue Hospital.

The President was moved into the improvised operating room, his mouth was disinfected time and again, and the operation was ready to begin.

Commodore Benedict and Secretary Lamont stayed on deck, out of the way. Except for the doctors, the only man in the main cabin was the ship's steward, who was to act as supply nurse.

The first job was to remove the teeth on the affected side of the President's mouth. Dr. Ferdinand Hasbrouck, the dentist, gave the President nitrous oxide, a mild anesthetic, and extracted the two left upper bicuspid teeth. Dr. Bryant then took over and made the incision on the roof of the mouth. Nitrous oxide was not an adequate anesthetic for the big man, as Dr. Hasbrouck had feared, and at 1:14 Dr. O'Reilly took over with ether. Another doctor kept close watch on the President's respiration and pulse, while Dr. Bryant continued the operation.

As he proceeded, he discovered that the ulcer on the surface was deceptively small, the entire jawbone was affected, and even the left antrum, the cavity in the upper jaw, was partly filled by a gelatinous mass of what appeared to be cancerous tissue. In the end, Dr. Bryant removed the entire left upper jaw, from the first bicuspid tooth to just beyond the last molar, and as far as the center line of the President's mouth.

He finished the operation at 1:55, packed the cavity with gauze to stop bleeding and allow the President to speak. Without the packing, his entire cheek was collapsed and his speech was unintelligible, but with the cavity stuffed he could be understood. The next day, weak but bright of eye, the President got out of bed for a few minutes, and on July 3, he was up and around.

Dr. Hasbrouck had left the yacht at New London, Connecticut, on July 2. The ship then turned across Long Island Sound, and put in at Sag Harbor on Long Island, where other doctors disembarked, although Dr. Bryant, who was known to the public as a friend as well as a physician, remained on board.

By this time the newspapers were becoming interested in the President's absence, for at most the trip from New York to Buzzards Bay should have taken only two days. On the morning of Independence Day the newspapers began speculating in sensational stories about the whereabouts of the President. Mrs. Cleveland talked to some newspapermen that day, saying there was no mystery, the President had decided to take a leisurely trip to the coast with his old friend and cribbage partner, Commodore Benedict.

The next day, July 5, the *Oneida* pulled into Buzzards Bay, and the President walked unassisted from the launch to his house, avoiding the newspapermen, who could see him however, and knew he was up and about.

On July 6 the newspapermen wanted to see Cleveland, but Lamont reported that the President was suffering from gout—rheumatism, he called it politely—and since the newspapermen knew that Cleveland had been afflicted with gout from time to time in recent years, they accepted the story, for a while.

It was remarkable that the secret could be kept so well, since so many different people, from doctors to the crew of the *Oneida*, knew at least part of the story. Actually, the word got out that the President had some kind of cancerous growth in his mouth, and in a few days a horde of newspaper reporters descended on Gray Gables.

This was what Secretary Lamont had come for. He met the newspapermen in an old barn about two hundred yards from the house and began to lecture them about frightening the American people.

It was foolish to make such a fuss over such a trivial matter, the Secretary said, but he would give them the whole story. The President was suffering from gout, but the reason for the prolonged voyage on the *Oneida* was that Mr. Cleveland had been suffering from dental troubles. Since the President had been so busy since his inauguration, he had not taken time to have his teeth treated. He had decided to combine an evil necessity with pleasure, and had brought the dentist on the yacht to take care of his teeth while they steamed to Massachusetts.

This explanation had a hollow and painful ring, but it did account for the presence of a dentist aboard the ship up to Massachusetts, and it did account for the President's sore mouth. Half the newspapermen swallowed the story, and the other half did not, but all had gone into the press conference with Lamont agreeing that they would accept a single story as the official version of the President's trip and would all file what was basically the same dispatch to their newspapers. They did so, and the rumors about the President's health began to subside.

But while the public was reassured, Dr. Bryant found real cause for worry. A few days after the President's arrival at Buzzards Bay, the doctor noticed what appeared to be malignant tissue in his daily examination of Cleveland's mouth. Apparently not all the cancerous growth had been cut out, and it must be cut out if the cancer was not to continue and spread. The doctors in New York were informed, and arrangements were made for them to come up to Buzzards Bay to carry out another operation. One night in the middle of July, four doctors took the train to Greenwich, Connecticut, boarded the *Oneida* again secretly, and sailed for Massachusetts.

When the *Oneida* arrived before Gray Gables, Cleveland embarked and set out for what appeared to be a pleasant cruise. But below deck, once again the President was on the operating table. This time Dr. Bryant removed all the suspicious tissue and cauterized the entire surface of the wound. The President returned to Gray Gables and to as much seclusion as he could manage to find.

The secret was fairly well kept because at no time had the doctors cut into the President's face. Both operations had been performed through the mouth, and since there was no scar, and the President could speak and looked well enough, although tired and thinner than usual, the newspapermen could not find any facts which would justify more than speculation on the state of the President's health.

While he rested at Gray Gables, one of the President's doctors fitted him with an artificial jaw of vulcanized rubber. This device supported the President's cheek and left his voice unaffected. The operation was over, the cancer had been cut out, and the cure was apparently complete.

Among the unknowing, the President came in for a considerable amount of criticism for leaving Washington at such a critical time in the nation's history. The bankers, particularly, were eager to have Congress assemble for they were desperate to have the Sherman Silver Purchase Act repealed and felt sure that calm heads in Congress would force the issue. They did not know that while the doctors were confident that they had removed the cancerous tissue, Cleveland himself felt that he was going to die. Still, he rallied his strength to prepare a message to be read to Congress when the special session assembled on August 7. The tone of the message would be extremely important, he knew, because he had taken a private poll of the attitudes of the men in the House of Representatives. He had learned that 173 of them were against the Sherman law, 114 of them were pro-silver men, and 69, who could swing the vote, were undecided.

One factor which worked in Cleveland's favor was the state of the silver market. All over the world the silver question was worrying governments, for the United States was not the only nation in the world to try a policy of bi-metallism. By the summer of 1893 the world price of silver had fallen very low—the law provided for the purchase of four and a half million ounces of silver every month, but did not force the treasury to buy silver if it was offered at a price above that of the world market. Much of the silver in the United States was offered at higher prices, so the treasury was not buying nearly four and a half million ounces a month.

Besides this, the silver camp was itself divided at this moment. The legislators from the mining states wanted the treasury to buy silver, stack it up in the treasury or bury it or mint it into coins—they did not care what the government did as long as it bought silver. The other silver men, who advocated bi-metallism as a matter of theory, wanted silver to be purchased only for coining. In other words, they wanted silver dollars to be equal to gold dollars, but they wanted the government to buy only as much silver as necessary to put into coins.

With the call for special session the silver men had begun rallying their forces, but in reality the issue had been obvious in Cleveland's selection of the cabinet and his first days in office. The silver men knew it was only a matter of time until the issue must be faced openly—an

issue which crossed party lines, for there were Republicans
in favor of unlimited silver coinage and Democrats who
favored it, too.

Among the Democrats who wanted to raise the importance of silver, the most pressing young man of all was
young Congressman William Jennings Bryan from Nebraska. Nebraska was a silver mining state, in a minor
way, but it felt akin to the mountain states which had a
huge stake in the future of silver. Bryan had supported
Grover Cleveland in 1884 and 1888, but by 1892 he had
begun to have his doubts about that choice, since Cleveland was opposed to the silver men. By 1893 Bryan accused the President of selling out to "the interests," which
meant the bankers of Wall Street, and set forth to oppose
the President, particularly on the money question. By the
time the members of Congress began to assemble in Washington in the first week of August, the silver men were
ready for a fight, and Bryan was aroused enough to dis-
tinguish himself as a promising leader of the silver bloc.
On August 7, when Cleveland's message to Congress demanded the outright repeal of the Sherman law, the battle
was ready to begin—a battle which would blight almost
the whole of the rest of Cleveland's second term and give
him a Congress more unfriendly to the President than
any since Andrew Johnson held the office after Lincoln's
assassination. .

✧ the struggle
for control

ON AUGUST 7, 1893, when President Cleveland's message
on silver was read to the assembled members of Congress,
the United States had almost reached the depths of the
depression which had harassed the nation all year. The
most startling part of this depression was the shortage of
money of any kind, even paper money. In New York City
some banks notified their depositors that they would have
to give sixty days notice if they wanted to withdraw any
money at all. Some other banks refused to give cash for
checks, offering certified bank checks instead. Some firms
which had originally paid debts in cash began paying by
check, and checks in many areas became more common
media of exchange than actual money. In some parts of
the country buyers and sellers were using scrip, and in
other areas they were actually using the barter system because money was in such short supply.

Several forces were at work in America: the resentment
of the western farmers and workmen against the moneyed
interests of the east, the resentment of labor against the
high-handedness and selfishness of employers, the feeling
that the country was dividing into classes, and the fear and
worry of severe economic depression. For the moment,
the problem of depression seemed foremost, and it was in

this atmosphere that President Cleveland's message was read to Congress.

Cleveland had forced himself to return to Washington for the opening of the special session, weak as he was, but he remained in Washington only five days before he went back to the coolness of Massachusetts.

On August 11 the administration's supporters began to make their arguments for the law which would repeal the silver purchase act. The arguments continued for more than two weeks; the most effective of them made by the young Nebraska Congressman William Jennings Bryan, who took the floor for the silver men to argue for the unlimited coinage of silver at the established ratio of sixteen ounces of gold equal to one ounce of silver in value. Bryan's appeal was the same as that of all the silver men: he argued that reduction in silver coinage kept money scarce and that by keeping money scarce the government favored the very rich and injured the workingman. The argument was not effective, however, because in a time when both gold and silver were being used, money was as scarce as it had ever been in the United States, and only a minority accepted the silver men's position that more silver was needed.

On August 28, despite the pleas of the silver men, the repeal bill passed in the house by a vote of 239 to 108. Cleveland had not only held all the hard money men and converted the fence-sitters, but he had changed the minds of some of the silver bloc as well. But in the Senate the bill faced greater trouble, for the Senate prided itself then, as now, as the greatest debating society in the world, and the silver men were determined to establish every possible argument and say every word that could be said.

The debate in the Senate began in August, moved through September, and was raging still in October. Two of the most vehement of the silver men, the senators from Nevada, owned silver mines themselves, which gave a sense of urgency to their arguments that might otherwise have been lacking. But personal involvement has never invalidated the right of a member of the Senate to argue, and argue these gentlemen did, most effectively. There was no question as to the outcome if the bill were brought up for a vote—the anti-silver forces would win by an enormous majority. But in the Senate, the right of unlimited debate is respected for being just what it says—unlimited. The silver men combined to raise every point of order, every debating device, to delay the vote. They hoped, by wearing down the opposition, to achieve a compromise measure, and they were very nearly successful. As the debate wore on, it created serious friction within the Democratic party. The silver men felt a kinship among themselves which surpassed party ties, and in the debating Democrats fell to insulting one another personally, passing words which would be remembered long after the details of the debate were forgotten.

Finally, in the last days of October, the silver men began a filibuster, a marathon of talk by which they hoped to force a compromise so that the other business of the legislative branch of the government might be considered. Nearly everyone in Washington was aching for a compromise, anything to end the interminable debate. One man alone stood flatly against compromise and for immediate repeal of the silver purchase act—Grover Cleveland. Amid sounds of distress from the newspapers and from Congress, Cleveland stood firm, and on October 30 he won his victory. The Senate passed the bill which outlawed silver purchases, by a vote of forty-eight to thirty-seven.

The Cleveland victory on monetary policy was a victory of principle, but it was to cost the President more perhaps than it was worth in the months to come. From the moment of his election Cleveland was pledged to the revision of the tariff. He believed in it, and he was determined that the McKinley tariff would be thrown out and a law which taxed luxuries more and necessities less would be enacted. In the winter of 1894, when Congress reconvened after the gruelling special session on the silver question, Cleveland began to press for the change in the tax on imported goods. The silver men had not recovered from their bitterness in the defeat on the money bill, and many of them joined the supporters of high tariffs.

Cleveland had also determined that in the Hawaiian affair Minister Stevens had acted far beyond his authority and had indeed subverted the Hawaiian monarchy of Queen Liliuokalani. It was impossible, as it turned out, to restore the monarchy because the queen cheerfully promised that she would execute President Dole and all the other American revolutionaries, and because the provisional government had become both popular and entrenched in the months of investigation and negotiation.

In opposition to imperialism, Cleveland antagonized another group in Congress, who also turned against him on issues that surpassed the bonds of political affiliation. Further, he antagonized a great number of Democratic politicians for his refusal to appoint men they wanted to government jobs; and in the argument in Congress about the tariff, he antagonized some Democratic members of both houses, who claimed that he was interfering with the rights of Congress. If there is any one action a President can take to create friction with his own party's legislators, it is to lead them to suspect that he is trying to assume legislative power, for Congress has always been exceedingly jealous of its own rights.

The result of all these complicated difficulties and disagreements was a gradual but growing loss of friendliness
and respect between the White House and Congress. In
the beginning of 1894, William L. Wilson, chairman of
the House Ways and Means Committee, and thus an important Democratic leader, introduced a tariff revision
measure which generally fitted the President's specifications. But both in the House and in the Senate the measure ran into difficulty, partly because the Republicans
were strongly in favor of high tariffs, partly because each
section of the country cared greatly about some imported
goods and not at all about others, and partly because of
the irritations Cleveland had stirred among the Congressmen.

The tariff fight dragged on for months—until the
end of July. When the tariff law was finally passed, it bore
little relation to the bill Cleveland had wanted. The high
tariff men slyly claimed that they had promised to revise
the tariff, not to lower it. Cleveland was sharp in his de-
nunciations of such dishonest tactics, but the nation was
exhausted by the struggle and was glad to have the issue
set aside, if not resolved. A number of newspapers pointed
out that the tariff cheapened the cost of living by lowering
the tax on a number of necessities. Yet several Democratic
state conventions endorsed the Cleveland position, and the
President, after much soul-searching, let the measure become a law without signing it. He might have vetoed the
bill, and he did consider vetoing it, but the shrinking
group of his supporters in Congress pleaded with him to
sign the bill as the best they could get through.

Cleveland was unhappy because in passing this bill,
which did change the trend of the tariff from high to low,
the Congress had taken the edge off the tariff issue with-

out really doing much about it. As passed, the tariff law would neither bring in much more revenue nor abandon the theory of protection in favor of stimulation of trade.

The money problem was not really solved by the end of silver purchases, because in the previous three years so many silver certificates had been issued that gold was constantly drained from the market. Everyone, it seemed, was hoarding gold, using the silver certificates to pay their debts, and taking silver certificates to the treasury to be redeemed in gold, as the federal government promised.

Early in 1894, even while he struggled with the tariff, Cleveland struggled also with the money problem. In the first seventeen days of January some eleven million dollars in gold were taken out of the treasury, and the gold reserve fell to sixty-nine million dollars. In January the treasury issued fifty million dollars in bonds to acquire more gold, but the drain continued. The silver men tried to pass a law to increase the coinage of silver, but Cleveland vetoed it because he felt there was already too much money—and particularly too much silver in circulation in the country. Silver was proving the old adage that "bad money drives out good" which had been repeated since the days when the Caesars multiplied their personal fortunes by debasing the coins of Rome.

Cleveland's veto was not understood by most people in the country, who were suffering even more from the depression than before, because none of the measures seemed to have brought the end of hard times that everyone had hoped. Actually, the United States was feeling a delayed reaction to the economic dislocations and excesses of the Civil War. Farmers had been overproducing wheat and most other crops during and after the war years; the railroads had expanded markets for a time, but the railroad owners and the other wealthy entrepreneurs had made of the years 1865-1890 a quarter century of unrestrained thievery on the public, and the nation was paying the bill.

As far as the workingman was concerned, the depression made itself felt in layoffs from factories and in pay cuts. In the spring, just after Cleveland vetoed the silver coinage bill, a giant strike occurred in the coal fields, affecting nearly two hundred thousand miners and coal workers. This strike was serious for the country, which heated with coal, and even more serious for the workmen, who had walked off their jobs in protest against low pay. But so depressed was the economy, and thus so easy was it for the employers to resist the strikers, that eventually men had to go back to work for the same wage they had refused before.

The shutting of factories and the strikes which plagued the country left a great army of men with time on their hands, dissatisfaction in their hearts, and no way to make their position felt except through mob action. A number of "armies" sprang up, not armies in the usual sense, but groups of unarmed men who banded together to try to call attention to their plight.

Chief among these armies was one organized in Massillon, Ohio, an industrial town which had been tortured by strikes and lockouts as much as any in the country. This army was called the Army of the Commonweal of Christ by its organizer, Jacob S. Coxey. On March 25, General Coxey and his force set forth from Massillon, bound for the steps of the Capitol in Washington, where they intended to make a demand that the government issue half a billion dollars in paper money. (Then no one thought about direct relief or government building projects to help the unemployed. Most people were convinced that all the government had to do to ease the depression was to put more money into circulation. They did not stop to consider the effect of indiscriminate issuance of money on the money that already existed, unless they were bankers or members of the wealthy class.)

General Coxey marched along on his road to Washington, making speeches and gathering adherents as he marched, until on May 1 he arrived in Washington. The nation had gone through many attitudes toward the army, even as Coxey marched. At first the army was regarded as a symbol of social unrest, and by labor leaders as proof that the government must provide work for the unemployed. But after five weeks the nation had grown tired of reading about Coxey, and when he arrived in Washington his loyal followers numbered just three hundred men. He carried his banners and his signs toward the Capitol steps, across the grass, and the police nabbed him for walking on the grass and threw him into jail. It was an ignominious end for a great crusade, for instead of calling attention to the plight of the working man, the Coxey march ended by bringing a welcome smile to the readers of newspapers. Less well publicized (Coxey had an army of forty-three newspaper correspondents in his train) were the armies of others. One, led by General Hogan, captured a Northern Pacific train, but the train was recaptured by soldiers and the nation again smiled.

Cleveland had little to smile about, however, for the entire nation seemed to be shifting nervously about, trying to find someone or something to blame for the evil state of affairs which continued month upon month: labor was organizing and the combinations of capitalists were organizing their forces to try to strangle the labor movement. The silver men of the west declared that Cleveland was their enemy, and the farmers and the working men began to believe that Cleveland was hand in hand with the bankers and industrialists of New York and Pennsylvania. Cleveland's health at this time was not as strong as it might have been, for he had been a long time in recovering from the cancer operation on his mouth. At the end of a busy spring he took a trip to the Caribbean on a lighthouse tender for a rest. It seemed to do him a world of good, for notwithstanding his girth, when the ship came in to port on the return voyage, he grandly vaulted over the rail while the gangplank was being lowered.

Cleveland believed in the strong use of power by the chief executive, and he did not hesitate to use all the powers he possessed in what he considered to be the national interest. He had moved against public opinion and the actions of his predecessor in the Hawaiian affair and had actually accused the American government of trampling on the rights of a tiny government. Yet in 1894, when Jose Zelaya established a dictatorship in Nicaragua, Cleveland failed to act with the kind of speed and decision the American people wanted, and his temporizing, in the face of the actual mistreatment of American interests, caused a great deal of unrest. The difference was emphasized by the British, who sent a warship and an occupation force of marines into Nicaragua to protect their interests. Americans wanted Cleveland to do the same, for Americans were ready for adventures outside the limits of the United States.

An old but true saying is that when trouble threatens at home, and domestic issues become almost unbearable, political leaders look abroad to pick a quarrel and cause a diversion. In the United States in 1894, however, the President was one of the few leaders who refused to look abroad for trouble. Congress and the other political leaders, including the lords of the press, were itching for diversion. They snarled at nearly every nation in Europe; they cast their eyes longingly on the tiny, weak republics and kingdoms of the world, particularly the island kingdoms. Since the nations of Europe were imperialist and kept acquiring colonies, why did not the United States do the same? Even Japan was bent on conquest, moving against Formosa and Korea, so why should the United States take such a holy attitude about the acquisition of an empire?

Cleveland resisted this super-nationalist sentiment and almost single-handedly prevented the United States from indulging in a foreign excursion, whether it was war or a colonial snatching of sovereignty. The temper of the United States definitely favored war—which was proved by the ease with which the nation was hurled into a disgraceful and totally unnecessary war against Spain two years after Cleveland's retirement from office. But in taking such a strong stand against imperialism, Cleveland lost popularity.

On the silver issue, many men believed Cleveland could have accomplished his aim, and yet kept the Democratic party united around him, by playing politics and accepting a compromise solution to the purchase puzzle. He refused to compromise, for as he told one of his leaders in the House of Representatives, what happened to his own position or to anyone else was of no concern as long as he was doing his best for the future of the nation.

The silver men had joined, regardless of party, to fight Cleveland, and the fight spread to almost every imaginable issue. In the congressional elections in the fall, the country, by and large, gave its opinion of the Democratic party and the administration. Naturally enough, Cleveland expected a fall in popularity, for no administration can remain popular in a depression. He had spent much of the late summer and early fall in Massachusetts, at the Buzzards Bay cottage, fishing, cutting trees for exercise, and then splitting them into firewood.

He did not return to Washington till just before election day and displayed not even the slightest interest in the outcome of the elections, much to the disappointment of his party leaders and to the infuriation of some of those in the west. It was a matter of mild interest perhaps that Representative William Jennings Bryan, who had chosen to run for the Senate from Nebraska that year, was defeated. But many Democrats were defeated—hardly a dozen members of the House were returned from all the states in the north and west, while the Populists and Republicans picked up seat after seat. The Republican majority in the House of Representatives would be more than two to one for the last two years of Cleveland's term. In addition, the leaders of the party held the President personally responsible for their defeats because of his refusal to act the politician and compromise issues to achieve political victories.

In this Cleveland seemed vastly unconcerned. He intended to complete his term, doing what he had done all along—following the course he thought was right.

✧ the pullman strike

FOR A POLITICAL LEADER who had risen to become President of the United States, Grover Cleveland was a remarkably simple and direct man. It is here, in the simplicity and straightforward nature of his character, that Cleveland has been misunderstood by contemporaries and even by historians, some of whom attributed great subtleties and hidden motives to a man whose record shows how unlikely it was that he would be capable of subtlety or any hidden motivation.

There is a word in the English language borrowed from the French which describes Cleveland as completely as a single adjective can ever characterize a man, and the word is *naive*. Unfortunately, in sophisticated twentieth century America the word naive has come to have overtones of gullibility and almost of stupidity. To understand the word and its key to Grover Cleveland's character one must return to the original Webster reference which defines the word as meaning unaffectedly simple, artless in the sense that he had no petty guile, and naturally honest. His life was simple and, quite unlike that of most Americans, had been lived largely in terms of the black and white of politics and the law, where an act is either legal or illegal and a policy is either right or wrong.

Cleveland possessed a genius for good government; a genius which usually was denigrated by the common belief that he offered nothing to government except a strong character, which from time to time bordered on bullheaded stubbornness. This attribute of his character, the strength of his ideals and the bluntness with which he followed them, is illustrated in the story of the great Pullman strike of 1894.

The industrial war between the powerful forces of the business community and the increasingly powerful forces of organized labor had caused bloody battles by 1894. In the coal mines and in the steel mills employers had locked workers out of factories and production lines in retaliation for actions the employers did not like, or simply when it became too costly to maintain production. The workers, on the other hand, were fed on a diet of propaganda and exhortation by their leaders, who knew that the best way to forge the links of a chain of organized labor was in the fire of industrial strife. Life was never quite so simple, of course, and the motivations of both sides were far more complex, depending in part on the rueful state of the depressed national economy, the growing feeling that classes had developed and that the working class could achieve its ends only by open warfare, the belief that all the apparent strength lay on the employers' side, and that the working man had strength only when he was united with his brothers.

Always, Cleveland took the position of referee between these factions, for it was his philosophy that the executive's task was to preserve the rights of the great amorphous public—60,000,000 Americans then—no matter what had to be done to preserve these rights, within the law. Cleveland spoke disparagingly of the "communism of combined wealth and capital," even more disparagingly than of the "communism of oppressed poverty and toil." For the communism of wealth, he said, was the outgrowth of "over-

weening cupidity and selfishness which assiduously under-
mines the justice and integrity of free institutions." Those
were strong words against the injustices of the employers,
but Cleveland, like many others, saw a growing tendency
toward development of a class society in America, and he
feared such a change, knowing that the capitalist could protect himself with the power of his money, but that the wage
earner was practically defenseless. Cleveland understood
the poor. So much is certain.

These views are important because they were announced
long before the Pullman strike, and in the strike his motives and his understanding were to be called into question.

Just outside Chicago, the Pullman Palace Car Company
had erected a model town next to the factories where it
made the sleeping cars used by now on most of the railroads
in the United States. George Pullman, the founder of the
company, had waged a long but finally successful battle
against the rival Wagner sleeping car company of the east,
and his Pullman company had achieved by 1894 a virtual
monopoly of the luxury and sleeping car traffic in the
United States. In his prosperity, Pullman conceived of the
idea of the model city, and the company erected houses,
stores, and other conveniences for the employees, in a burst
of baronial paternalism. Establishment of the model town
was expensive, however, and when it came time to rent the
houses to the workers, the company discovered that its interests would be served only by charging higher rents than
workers paid for housing in Chicago. The housing in the
Pullman village was better housing, but for that matter the
workers were given no choice. The houses and the rents
were both fixed.

About five thousand men and their families lived in
the company town, and about four thousand of the men
were members of the American Railway Union, an organi-

zation founded by labor leader Eugene V. Debs in 1893 as
a reaction to popular distaste for the railroad brotherhoods.
The American Railway Union grew rapidly, and within a
year had a membership of 150,000 men. It was a strong
union, and it was ready to back the demands of its members. For the most part these demands were likely to be
radical, for the union leadership was made up of discon-
tented, fretful men.

In the slack period of the depression, the Pullman company reduced the wages of the workmen by about twenty-
five percent. The company was profitable: in 1893 it had
paid an average dividend of seven percent. The wage re-
ductions were made to be sure the company remained
profitable and that an equal dividend might be paid to
capital investors in the year 1894.

Wage reduction was bad enough, but the high rents and
other costs were not reduced by the company. The workmen, then, were caught squarely in the middle. A group of
them went to see Pullman after the hard winter and asked
that wages be raised or that the rents be lowered. Pullman
refused to do either, and while he promised there would be
no reprisals against the men who had made the request,
three of the group were discharged almost immediately.
The union men went out on strike, and on this action the
company closed its shops and threw the other thousand
workers out of jobs.

President Debs of the American Railway Union coun-
selled temperance. The national convention of the union,
meeting in Chicago, voted to seek arbitration of the dispute, but the Pullman company would not arbitrate. Then
the union voted a boycott against all Pullman cars, which
put the union in direct conflict with twenty-three railroads
operating in twenty-seven states. The union men chose a
formidable opponent—for in fact they still had one oppo-

nent, the railroad industry. The affected railroads were organized in what was called the General Managers' Association. This association had resisted the demands of labor as much as possible through the years. Now, as it was later determined, the General Managers' Association set out to crush union labor on the railroads once and for all. There was to be no nonsense about conciliation, arbitration, or mediation. The strike was to be brought to an end by driving the strikers to their knees, and, if possible, destroying the American Railway Union.

Debs appealed to the strikers to refrain from any violent acts, but the strikers, worn down by months of national depression, and sensing, if not knowing, the full extent of employer resistance, began to harass train crews and track repairmen. In Chicago 20,000 trainmen quit work, and another 40,000 went out along the western lines.

On June 28, two days after the railroads were struck, the newspapers reported it was the greatest battle between labor and capital in history. In Chicago, a jittery post office reported that the mails were completely obstructed. On June 29, the strikers stopped a New York bound train at Hammond, Indiana, and forced the crew to take off two Pullman cars; and two other trains had been delayed in Chicago by strikers. Governor John Altgeld of Illinois, a man friendly to labor, did not feel that the situation was dangerous enough to interfere, but in Washington, Cleveland received quite another story.

Probably no one will ever know the full extent of the influence Attorney General Richard Olney exerted on President Cleveland in the Pullman strike. Cleveland took full responsibility for his own actions, but from the beginning, his vision was clouded, first by the exaggerated reports which appeared in the newspapers, and second by Olney's prejudice in favor of the employers. Olney had been a railroad lawyer for years, and his personal philosophy favored the rights of property over the rights of individuals. He determined that he would use the injunction power of the courts to stop the strike, and when that failed, as he was sure it would fail, he would persuade Cleveland to call in federal troops to stop the strike. It was in effect, a plan by the vigorous, misguided Olney to serve the cause in which he believed.

Four thousand United States marshals were sent to the railroad staging areas to preserve order and keep the mails moving, and Olney appointed a special U.S. attorney named Edwin Walker to present a plea for an injunction against the strikers.

Olney's choice was less than disinterested. Walker was attorney for the Milwaukee Road, one of the railroads in the fight, and his basic interest was not that of justice, but to serve the railroad owners. The injunction was obtained, and then the marshals tried to enforce it.

At that moment the strike was in reality over, as Debs said later, because it put the strikers in the position of violating the law if they disturbed the trains in any way. Olney, however, was not satisfied, and through a series of urgent telegrams succeeded in getting his Chicago men aroused to the point where they sent a telegram filled with rumor, misinformation, and innuendo to the Attorney General—saying that mob rule threatened the entire Chicago area.

There had been talk at the White House about the use of federal troops before, but half the President's advisors (including the military men) did not want to send in troops. Olney, and only Olney, was the guiding force. When he appeared at a cabinet meeting on July 3 and waved his sensational telegram about the room, all opposition vanished. To Cleveland the issue was, as usual, black and white. He was sworn to uphold the law and to keep the mails and interstate transportation in order, and the strike threatened both. The injunction had been issued and the further duty of the federal government was to enforce the rulings of the federal judge.

The troops were called out and ordered to Chicago to establish martial law.

It was not all one-sided. The strikers did damage—an officer was stabbed outside Chicago when the marshals tried to put down a mob; some sources have estimated the property loss (and this, of course includes income) at $10,000,000 from the strike. The nation, generally speaking, was behind Cleveland when he called out the troops. The strikers were regarded as dangerous radicals. The newspapers fostered that view, and there was much fear of the unknown evils of anarchy in the land.

In Chicago, the strikers were nearly out of control. Union President Debs talked excitedly about civil war, and the tensions mounted. Finally on July 5 and July 6 the troops and strikers met in combat, and on July 7 there was a skirmish in which seven men were killed.

The government moved rapidly then. President Debs and several others were arrested and indicted for obstructing the United States mails. Cleveland issued an order that there was to be no unlawful assemblage—in other words he sent the people to their houses and told them to stay there.

Governor Altgeld protested this invasion of state sovereignty by the federal executive branch, but Cleveland paid no heed. It was typical of him that he had been slow to decide on direct action. He did not want to send in troops, and would not have done so, had he not been misinformed by his Attorney General, whose motives were scarcely disinterested. But having made up his mind, the President would not be dissuaded by the arguments of others. He sent in the troops, quelled the strike, and brought order back to the railroads.

The strike collapsed when Debs and the other union leaders were put in jail—or really, as noted, with the government injunction forbidding the stopping of trains or interference with the railroads in their delivery of the mails. The men might have stayed out, refusing to work, but their weapons were gone and the only course would have been further disaster and starvation. The strike was broken, the union collapsed, and the entire American labor movement suffered a blow which was temporarily crippling, but in the end was to result in such tight union control of railroads that the operators would feel crippled and put upon.

Cleveland was not totally satisfied with the results of his own action, and on July 26 he ordered an investigation by an impartial commission. The commissioners interviewed one hundred and nine witnesses in and around Chicago and found that while the company had assumed the right to fix wages and rent absolutely and had done all possible to repress labor in the Pullman shops, still the strikers had broken the law. Twelve people had been killed, five hundred and fifteen had been arrested, and seventy-one men had been indicted under federal law.

Debs and his companions were convicted of breaking the federal law—interfering with the mails. Debs went to jail for six months, and several others for three months, to become labor martyrs in the end.

Cleveland's course was approved almost uniformly for a time, but some newspapers and political leaders, particularly in the south, where they were very conscious of states' rights, did not approve. The governor of Texas wired Cleveland during the strike and told him he would handle any problems that arose in Texas—that Cleveland could keep his federal troops out of the Lone Star State. Cleveland also became an outright target for organized labor, whose members condemned the President at one mass meeting after another.

Had he given more consideration to the politics involved in his action, and less to the demands of conscience, Cleveland would not have played so completely into the hands of the railroad barons as he did in breaking the strike for them. Governor Altgeld, who understood the situation better than Cleveland, later announced that he had been willing to throw a hundred thousand state troops into Chicago if the need arose. He had not so indicated, however, and had not discussed the matter with the President. Unfortunately the President did not feel it incumbent on him, in his office, to discuss the question of federal and state responsibilities by using the telephone, as he might have done. The result was another demonstration of Cleveland's strength of character, but also a show of the ignoble uses that character could serve, when he was duped into hasty action by his advisors. The strike of 1894 showed Cleveland in his weakest position: that of the man of principle who is not pliable enough.

✿ the venezuelan affair

IT IS QUITE PLAIN that the years of 1893 and 1894 with the struggle over silver, the tariff, and the Pullman strike had established a new image of Grover Cleveland as President, not just one image but two, depending on the region in which the observer lived and his economic station.

After the Pullman strike and the disastrous elections, the silver men, both Republican and Democrat, became loud in their denunciation of Cleveland as the creature of the "interests," which meant banker J. P. Morgan and the other wealthy business moguls of the east. Among the Silver Democrats, Cleveland was regarded as the greatest liability in the history of the party. They were certain they could not win the election, even in 1894, unless they shook the President's shadow from their coattails. William Jennings Bryan, for example, spent as much time during the campaign excoriating the President as he did in arguing against his opponent for the Nebraska Senate seat. When he was defeated, he became editor of the Omaha *Herald,* the most important daily newspaper in his state, which gave him a podium from which to carry on the fight against Cleveland and for silver. Already, Bryan was looking for more of a future in the Democratic party than a Senate seat would have given him. He saw himself as an important leader, which in effect, he was, because the other western leaders were growing old and ineffectual while Bryan was travelling the Chautauqua discussion circuit, haranguing the eager crowds with the story of silver, and meeting organization Democrats in every region of the country.

Cleveland's part in the Pullman strike was generally applauded, and in the eyes of the more conservative in the nation he became more popular than before, because he had again emphasized the strength of character for which he had been elected originally. The images of Cleveland were formed by 1894, but they were to be solidified in the next two years in two actions—the bond issue of 1895 (which is sometimes referred to scathingly as the Morgan bond issue) and the Venezuela boundary case.

At the end of 1894 it was apparent that nothing the government had done to improve the state of the money market had been effective for long. Gold was being hoarded, and as long as the federal government continued to pay off all paper obligations in gold, there was no recourse to the constant depletion. The silver men argued that the government need not continue to pay obligations in gold, but that the nation at large would be pleased enough to receive the payment in silver. This argument was true of the workers and farmers and debtors, but it was not true of the bankers and the moneyed class, and more important to Cleveland, the abandonment of a single gold standard would have an unknown effect on the American government's financial position vis-à-vis Europe.

Perhaps Cleveland did not have much imagination in his failure to see that the situation of 1894 and 1895 played squarely into the hands of the moneyed interests. But one must recall that the entire national banking and financial structure of that period lay in those same hands, that few in the past had questioned the system, and that the revolt of the silver men represented a radical break with the past and with the traditional concept of money as an absolute, solid medium of exchange. In the European and American concepts of money in those days, gold had an absolute value, and all other money was based on gold.

Cleveland never solved the money problem: he was in no position to outlaw silver, particularly when his own party turned against him at the beginning of his second term, and in the mid-term elections the Congress slipped into Republican hands; and he would not go the other way and take the nation off the gold standard. Each year, (because of these factors), the treasury's position grew more desperate. By the fall of 1894 the gold in the treasury amounted only to about sixty million dollars.

Because the depression continued and grew worse, the federal government was not securing anything like the amounts of the past in tariff revenues, and instead of a surplus, in 1894 the government had a deficit of nearly seventy million dollars. It was a complete reversal of the situation Cleveland faced in his first administration. By February 1, 1895, there was only $41,000,000 in gold left in the treasury, and worse, the New York sub-treasury, which handled the government's business with Wall Street, had scarcely enough of a gold reserve to last another working day at the current rate of withdrawals. The moneyed men were systematically milking the United States Treasury of gold to increase their own fortunes at the expense of the American taxpayers.

For several weeks before February 5, Cleveland and his Secretary of the Treasury had been meeting with J. Pierpont Morgan and August Belmont to see what might be done to shore up the government's shaky finances. Cleveland wanted to put out another bond issue to the general public, but the bankers said it would be extremely risky, for the public confidence was shaky, and if the public did not buy up the bonds quickly enough, their value on the open market would fall, and thus the entire issue, plus all previous issues of bonds, might be endangered. The only possible solution, Morgan said, was for a group of bankers to subscribe to the bonds themselves, pay the government, and then market them slowly or hold them, without letting the price drop.

The trouble with Morgan's solution, from the Cleveland point of view, was that the bankers wanted far too high a price for doing this service to their government (and saving their own fortunes). Cleveland stalled, hoping that Congress would come to his aid, or that the bankers could be forced down in their demands.

Morgan went to Washington on February 7, and immediately became angry because Cleveland refused to see him that evening. He was forced to spend an extra evening in Washington rather than get back to his own comfortable mansion in New York. He spent the night—until four in the morning—playing solitaire in a room in the Arlington Hotel, talking to treasury officials, and growing more irritable by the hour.

The next day, Cleveland met with Morgan. The Congress had refused him the day before, by voting down a bill on which Cleveland had counted to solve the problem. There were some legal problems which bothered the President, but his aides had found answers to them, and in the end, the President yielded to give the financiers their private bond issue, convinced that there was no other course. The clinching factor was the information that only $9,000,-000 existed in the sub-treasury in New York, and Morgan announced that he knew of the existence of a $12,000,000 check outstanding at that moment which would throw the government into bankruptcy if it were presented and could not be paid.

Morgan further promised that he would make sure that the tremendous drain of gold to Europe would be stopped (which later aroused unpleasant thoughts that Morgan and the other bankers had more than a minor responsibility for that drain).

The bargain was concluded, the government received sixty-two million dollars in gold and was saved; and Morgan and company made some seven million dollars in the transaction, partly because the price they had established was so high, and partly because the securities *were* readily salable to the public. Cleveland came in for a great deal of renewed criticism from the silver men for giving away the country's wealth, but what other recourse did he have? He had been abandoned by a Congress which refused to take action to save the gold currency Congress itself had ordered; his only recourse was to take the Morgan bargain, bad as is was, or stop payment in gold and take the nation off the gold standard, a move he could not conscientiously make, given his belief in gold.

The story of the Venezuela boundary dispute put Cleveland in a different light, and showed how even he was becoming afflicted in some ways by that itchy feeling for expansion and involvement in world affairs that was known in the period as "manifest destiny." This strong pair of words meant that the United States was destined to become a force in world affairs, so why should not the United States act like the big European powers and begin acquiring an empire and imposing its national strength around the world?

The sense of growing power and the demand for world recognition of it had been shown in the attempt by the Harrison administration to annex Hawaii. Cleveland had put an end to that attempt at annexation; although he could not return Hawaii to the control of Queen Liliuokalani, he had refused to make the islands a part of the United States and left them as an island republic, independent and alone. The Hawaiian affair was not finished; it would not again become a major issue in Cleveland's administration, but his decision had not been popular, since the feeling in the land was expansionist and super-nationalist.

When Cleveland had first become chief executive, one of the international problems which had bothered him was the unsettled boundary between Venezuela and British Guiana, a boundary which had never been fixed. When he returned to office in 1893, the boundary still had not been fixed, and Venezuela was growing somewhat restive under the situation. Americans were becoming more restive, because the British gave every indication of encroaching on the Orinoco River, which would mean that the British would control trade in this area of the interior of South America. Such an idea did not appeal to American businessmen who were interested in South America, nor did it appeal to the American government, which was conscious, although not overly conscious, of the lasting promise of the Monroe Doctrine against European interference in the western hemisphere.

In 1894, Cleveland told Congress he hoped to settle the Venezuela issue soon, and asked the British to submit the matter to arbitration. The British foreign office, however, was not anxious to reply. In the spring of 1895 Cleveland felt that the British had been given quite enough time to answer, and they had not.

The dispute had grown very complicated, because it had continued for so long. In 1814 the British had acquired three provinces of Dutch Guiana and had turned them into an independently governed colony. Not until 1840 was an English engineer named Robert Schomburgk sent to survey the boundary, and when he had finished the British prepared to accept that as their line, but the Venezuelans would not agree. Both sides had encroached on the no-man's land in the area from time to time without serious incident, but with notices passed back and forth that neither side accepted the claims of the other to the land.

By now Venezuela wanted to arbitrate, but the British would not discuss the matter.

Cleveland became more and more annoyed as the summer wore on, and finally in the fall he sent a very severe note to the British, demanding action, and calling attention to the Monroe Doctrine (but in a way which seemed to raise some question about Britain's relations with Canada and her other colonies in the Caribbean).

The British government was heavily occupied in disputes elsewhere: in South Africa and in the Middle East. No answer came at all, so in the winter of 1895 Cleveland decided that the United States would establish a commission and set a boundary to settle the dispute.

"In making these recommendations I am fully alive to the responsibility incurred, and keenly realize all the consequences that may follow," the President said. It did not need much interpretation of that sentence for a reader to realize that Mr. Cleveland was talking about the possibility of war with Britain, and saying that he accepted that danger cheerfully.

When the message to Britain was released in the United States, most people were delighted. They felt it was time the United States gave a show of strength.

Congress immediately appropriated $100,000 for the establishment of the boundary commission—and recalling how bad were Cleveland's relations with Congress by this time it was a remarkable show of support. A number of senators, Democrats and Republicans, spoke on the Senate floor in favor of the President's action. The popular and partisan press was quick to support the move.

There was, however, a speedy reaction by sober heads who realized that the tiny American navy—which had been useless when Cleveland first came to office—was no match for the British fleet.

Cleveland went ahead, however, and to everyone's surprise there were no ill effects. The British, instead of declaring war, appeared shocked that matters had come to such a crisis and were surprisingly friendly in agreeing to arbitrate the dispute. The reaction in Great Britain was surprise that the United States could have become so aroused about such a minor matter, and this reaction was followed by a sudden realization that Americans were more annoyed with British policies in the Americas than her majesty's government had ever thought they might be.

A few years later a Republican President, Teddy Roosevelt, would make history by adopting a truculent attitude and talking of walking softly but carrying a big stick; but Cleveland had drawn the attention of the world to the growth of America as a world force, and he had forced the British to relent from their preoccupation with imperial problems enough to pay attention to her relations with the United States. Before the era of Cleveland, the United States was looked upon as a nation which had no interests beyond its territorial borders, except such undisturbing interests as freedom of the seas from piracy. The United States, as a nation, had shown no particular interest in any part of the world. European involvements, even in Latin America, had gone unhailed or unchided, save when they involved American interests directly. In the Venezuela border case American interests were not involved directly, and yet the President and United States had been disturbed enough to send a stern message to Great Britain, which might possibly result in war. The result was a new world respect for the American government, and the realization by European nations that here was a new power that would have to be considered in their conduct of world affairs.

☆ silver and gold—
from the sidelines

GROVER CLEVELAND had one great deficiency, more a failing of personality than of character: in person he was warm-hearted, responsive, sensitive, and in every way a good friend; as a public official he was so filled with a sense of responsibility for the importance of public office that he was overly sober, even to the point of seeming tiresome. He had no gift for picturesque speech, such as that of Teddy Roosevelt. Cleveland even appeared to be habitually solemn where Roosevelt always seemed to be grinning. Cleveland was a father figure to the nation, portly and stern, respected but loved only in a detached way, and by the end of his second term in office he had led the country to believe he was old-fashioned.

Cleveland *was* old-fashioned in his consideration of two important ideas of the period. One of these, of course, was silver. By 1896 the majority of the Democratic party had been persuaded that silver should be made a partner of gold money at the fixed ratio of sixteen to one, that silver should be coined unrestrainedly to increase the supply of money in the market, and that in every way silver should be "as good as gold," in ratio of course. Cleveland saw the silver issue as the second great issue of his era, even greater than the tariff, and nearly as great as the issue of slavery just before the Civil War. The Democratic party had taken the wrong side on slavery and had not elected a President for twenty-eight years thereafter because of that position. Cleveland was sure the silver issue would prove as serious an issue and as destructive to the Democratic party as slavery.

The second important idea, favored by the Republicans but not by any sizeable segment of the Democratic party, was imperialism. Americans were well enough in control of their own continent—or thought they were—that the idea of foreign adventure appealed to them. The newspapers drummed constantly in favor of annexation of foreign islands and possessions, and the whole cause was aided immeasurably by the requests by factions within various little dependencies who asked for annexation by the United States. Each time such a report swept across the nation it left behind a trail of excitement and speculation. Accompanying this interest was a long resentment against Europe and its ways, particularly against the nations which had their hands in the original settlement of the North American continent, and especially Britain and Spain, which maintained colonial possessions very near the boundaries of the United States.

Had Cleveland been a man of ready public wit, perhaps his attitudes would have had more influence on those of his party and the nation. His public statements reflected the clarity and brilliance of high principle, but except when he had his neck bowed against some oppressor or some wrong, his statements did not appeal to the public imagination. Speaking on the danger of letting the Republicans become the party in favor of sound money, Cleveland wrote this:

"If we should be forced away from our traditional doctrine of sound and safe money, our old antagonists will take the field on the platform which we abandon, and neither the votes of reckless Democrats nor reckless Republicans will avail to stay their easy march to power."

The statement was sound, and the prediction was uncannily accurate, but Americans, and particularly Democrats, were much more attracted to the mellifluous tones of the voice of William Jennings Bryan. When he spoke of the plight of the poor and the cunning of the bankers of the east, he made it quite apparent to his listeners (until they left the range of his voice, at least) that free silver was the lifeline for the one and the cudgel for the other.

By 1895 Bryan had become important enough in Democratic party councils that his brand of party politics was dignified by the term Bryanism, which referred to advocacy of free silver, strict control of business, strict regulation of the railroads, and neutralism in world affairs. Among the business people, particularly in the east, there was much talk of running Cleveland for a third term, but Cleveland was flatly determined that he would not consider a third term under any circumstances. His announced determination made no difference to Cleveland's political enemies, who accused him of attempting to create a dynasty. Where these tactics were successful, they produced more strength for the silver forces.

In the west, the south, and the middle west, the silver men were well organized and took control of the Democratic organizations, financed by the mining men of the mountain states. When it came time for the Democratic convention of 1896 in Chicago, the silver men had more than a majority of delegates, although they were not certain of the two thirds majority it would take, by tradition, to nominate a candidate for the Presidency. The sound money men hoped to push through a plank in the party platform which would call for the maintenance of the gold standard, but they were not at all sure they would be able to do so. The silver men were confident that they could force through a plank which called for the unlimited coinage of silver.

That year the Republican convention met in St. Louis a few days before the Democrats were to meet, and the Republicans came out in favor of the gold standard before nominating William McKinley, author of the McKinley tariff law, for the Presidency. It was as Cleveland had predicted; the Republicans were picking up the torch of sound money, and the Republicans were united on the subject, because the silver Republicans, led by Senator Teller of Colorado, had walked out of the party on this issue.

The stern Cleveland was always unresponsive to public opinion; it had been one of his greatest self-made disabilities all his political life. In the fight on the tariff, his friends said he might have resolved the issue had he spoken out six months before he did speak; on the silver fight his friends also said he might have lessened the party split by speaking up sooner. Now, while the third term rumors spread around the country, Cleveland refused to make a public statement that he was not a candidate—not because he had any intention of changing his mind, but because he did not want to dignify rumors.

A week before the Chicago convention Cleveland left the White House very early in the morning, bound for his summer home on Buzzards Bay and vacation. It would have been very unusual if he had travelled to the convention, for as leader of the party and leader of the nation, it would be unseemly for him to engage in open political maneuvering.

When the Democratic convention opened in Chicago on July 7, the men who favored the gold standard counted on Cleveland's influence to maintain the President's monetary policies. But Cleveland's influence had fallen very low. He had argued and struggled with too many Democratic leaders for too long, over everything from postmasterships to the tariff. From the beginning the silver men were in control. They elected the officers of the convention; they passed their silver plank; and they nominated their silver candidate, William Jennings Bryan, who had told the convention: "You shall not press down upon the brow of labor this crown of thorns. You shall not sacrifice mankind upon a cross of gold."

Cleveland even received a slap by the convention. A resolution had been offered, as was usual, by the party whose chief was the President of United States, commending the current administration. However, the Democratic convention of 1896 defeated the resolution praising its own President, Grover Cleveland. The insult was deliberate and complete. Further, at the convention, Bryan came out against the intervention by federal forces in state matters— this was a direct condemnation of Cleveland's use of troops in the Pullman strike in Chicago.

This excess of Bryanism was a serious error on the part of the Democrats. Cleveland had no intention of supporting Bryan or the party platform, for the Democrats had made that impossible but, in insulting the President, the Democrats alienated many voters, Democrats and Republicans, who were strong admirers of the President. In truth, the Democrats over-estimated the feelings for silver or against Cleveland's strict policies within the country at large. Chauncey Depew, a leading Republican and head of the New York Central Railroad, had noted the temper of most Americans earlier in the year. Worrying over Cleveland as a possible opponent for the Republicans, he said the President would be hard to defeat, even if the unpopularity of the third term issue could be used against him.

Probably it was inevitable, but the insults of the regular Democrats and the silver issue brought about the formation of a new party, composed almost completely of Democrats from forty-one states. They met in Indianapolis and nominated Senator John M. Palmer of Illinois for the Presidency. They had offered the nomination to Cleveland but he had refused, flatly and definitely. Cleveland wrote the new party leaders that he was delighted to mingle with those who were determined that "the voice of true Democracy shall not be smothered." Cleveland planned to make that his single public statement in the entire campaign. He was drawn out a time or two more, but that was all.

Cleveland understood, when he threw his support to the Gold Democrats, that he was helping split the party and helping William McKinley to victory. He understood that, and he favored it, for between Bryan and McKinley he would have favored McKinley every time.

What had come about in the last few years to drive such a wedge between the President and his party?

The fault was not Cleveland's in matters of principle. He had not changed nor had he wavered. His faults were errors in grace, not in honesty or purpose, and while the errors had caused considerable pain to Democratic politicians, by themselves Cleveland's actions in matters of patronage and party etiquette would not have made so drastic a change.

The important change was in the Democratic party itself, particularly in its strength in the growing west and midwest areas, and in the south, where farmers and working men wanted cheap money, and the mining men were willing to pay for the campaign.

The campaign was a one-sided affair: McKinley sat on his front porch in Canton, Ohio, and greeted visiting delegations, and Bryan toured the nation by train and buggy, speaking almost constantly each day from noon to sundown. In October, Cleveland said he was sure Bryanism was on the wane. When the election was over McKinley had won handily, and Bryan and a great number of Republicans gave Cleveland credit for the McKinley victory. Those who thought Cleveland a traitor to his party for deserting so completely seemed to have forgotten that they had censored him out of the party in Chicago. The political issue of free silver died with the campaign of 1896, and although it was to be brought into the campaign of 1900, times had changed and by then the voters were not impressed. Cleveland had lost, but he had won a great victory on monetary policy.

In dealing with the second great movement which colored the last days of Cleveland's administration, the story was not at all the same. There was no bitterness, but rather a constant development of the idea of imperialism and involvement with foreign affairs by the American people, and a constant resistance of imperialism by Cleveland.

In 1895 the Spanish colony of Cuba had rebelled against the mother country. It was not the first such rebellion, but it was to be the last one, for this time a million and half Cubans, white, Indian, and Negro, were willing to burn their fields and homes and fight to the death to force the Spanish to leave the island.

The Spanish had never been overly kind to the natives of their colonies. Before the rebellion it was Spanish practice to levy heavy taxes on the people of Cuba, and then, if the Cubans were accused of failure to pay or of other breach of the laws, to chop them to death with machetes. When the rebellion began, the Spanish garrison commanders created huge concentration camps and thrust hundreds of thousands of suspects into them, to die of disease, starvation, or an attempt to escape under Spanish guns.

American interests were involved because, even then, nearly fifty million dollars of American money was invested in Cuba, but equally important, American sympathies were involved so much that Cleveland considered offering

the Spanish government a hundred million dollars for
Cuba, if some way could be found to establish the independence of the island and secure repayment of the money.
Other Americans, including a strong group in Congress,
wanted to declare war on Spain and annex Cuba to the
United States. Cleveland grew very angry at that last sug-
gestion.

"There will be no war with Spain over Cuba while I am
President," he said.

One Congressman flushed and told the President that he
had forgotten that Congress had the right to declare war.
He had not forgotten that fact, the President said, but he
was commander-in-chief of the armed forces, and he would
refuse to mobilize the army.

Cleveland tried to mediate the dispute, but the Spanish
government cut him off, saying that their political system
was one of the most liberal in the world and that they would
not budge from their government's position, nor would
they make any concessions to the revolutionaries.

The dispute was left unresolved then, for Cleveland
could not mediate it in that spring of 1897, and it would
have to remain for President McKinley to deal with.

The day on which Cleveland would leave the White
House and President McKinley would move in drew closer.
Cleveland kept at work at his desk, but tried to leave the
new chief executive as much room for maneuvering as possible, since the problems, Cuba among them, would not be
his to resolve, but would fall to McKinley. Cleveland was
looking forward with eagerness to his own retirement from
public life at the age of sixty. Soon he would be able to hunt
and fish as much as he wished while he brought up his children.

The children had been the deciding factor in Cleveland's
selection of a permanent home. Again, he had not seriously

considered Buffalo—it had too many unpleasant memories for him. He did consider New York City, but abandoned the idea of living in the city when he thought of bringing up his three daughters there. Finally, he and Mrs. Cleveland bought a house in Princeton, New Jersey, where they would make their home.

On the evening of March 3, President-elect McKinley came to the White House to dine, the two political leaders exchanged warm greetings and spent a pleasant evening together, for they were united in one matter at least—both favored the gold standard and both had fought against Bryan and the silver men to keep the gold standard in force.

The next day, March 4, was a clear and cloudless morning, unusual for an inauguration day in Washington—so unusual that Cleveland took his umbrella to the capitol in spite of the sunny sky. There he stood quietly as William McKinley was inaugurated as President of the United States. Then he left the podium, after a few brief words with McKinley, and drove to the dock on the Potomac river, where a steamer waited to take him on a two week hunting trip, the cares of high office forever behind him.

✯ the last years

THE GROVER CLEVELAND who settled in Princeton two weeks after he retired from the Presidency bore little resemblance to the Grover Cleveland who had spent the last sixteen years, with a four-year respite, in the wearing grind of public office. During his tenure as President, Cleveland had been a stern and uncompromising figure. He would accept none but the most trivial of gifts; he refused honorary degrees with a sense of false modesty which concealed a bit of contempt and a fear that the officials who offered him something for nothing would later ask favors.

Now he accepted honorary degrees; he was available to all acquaintances in the study on the second floor of the big old-fashioned house; and he welcomed visitors from the college and from the town when they came to call. He ordered a pony for his children, and when the pony came, he dropped all his work to spend the entire day playing with them. His anger, these days, was released in little bursts, perhaps at the fish in Buzzards Bay when they refused to appear, or his launch, which worked so badly that he kept threatening never to go out in her again. Having retired from politics, he contented himself, for a time, with watching dispassionately—or as dispassionately as he could watch the disintegration of his old party—from the sidelines.

He was very happy in the stone and stucco mansion, surrounded by a loving wife and his three daughters, and happier still when his first son, Richard Folsom Cleveland, was born that same year.

Cleveland was elected a trustee of Princeton University, and later became chairman of the board of trustees, a position in which he had many associations with Woodrow Wilson, then president of the university. Cleveland and Wilson disagreed on several college matters, and eventually the sharp-tongued Wilson turned entirely against Cleveland. Yet the remarkable point was that even in their sharpest disagreements Wilson had no fault to find with Cleveland's intellect, but rather with his point of view. This was more than remarkable, considering Wilson's extremely critical attitude toward most other men.

Cleveland's life was quiet, and yet no President can ever remain totally aloof from the affairs of the nation, affairs in which his formulation of policies could not be forgotten. When Cleveland left the White House, the threat of war with Spain seemed very great. Nevertheless, Cleveland had believed that war could be averted if he would stand firm against the ultra-nationalists in Congress. Even on his last day as President, this matter had been uppermost in his mind. As he took his leave of McKinley that day, he again mentioned the need for firmness in the Spanish situation.

President McKinley, however, was a man of an entirely different mind, and the Republicans were overwhelmingly in favor of a war—a war "for the benefit of humanity." On April 25, 1898, after the sinking of the battleship *Maine* in Havana harbor, Congress did declare war on Spain, with the consent of President McKinley.

Even after the *Maine* disaster, Cleveland was outspoken in his feeling that it would be outrageous to declare war on Spain, for he did not believe that the manner in which Spain chose to treat Cuba, her colony, was any more the business of the United States than it was the business of Spain to interfere if, for example, the United States government took some action that the people of Florida did not like.

Cleveland was out of touch with the times, some said, but while that was true it made no difference to Grover Cleveland, for he had never yielded a whit to the opinion of newspaper publishers or letter writers. Once his course was clear to himself, he followed the course faithfully, no matter where it might lead, whether to political defeat for the Presidency in the tariff battle of 1888 or to political outlawry from the Democratic party as in the silver battle of 1896. The former President said there was no reason for war, and even after war was declared he remained firm in his belief that it was unnecessary and disgraceful. Yet once the action was taken, Cleveland felt that as a member of the American public he had no course but to support the government in the war in every way he could.

The war was distasteful enough, but Cleveland was more worried about the spirit of imperialism which accompanied it. The United States, he felt, had enough unfinished business at home to keep Americans occupied, without exerting effort and taking the new responsibility for annexing islands and adding new populations with different cultures and different problems.

Strangely enough, at this point Cleveland and William Jennings Bryan found themselves in agreement, for Bryan, too, opposed imperialism and managed to work an anti-imperialist plank into the Democratic platform in 1900 when he was renominated.

That community of interest was not great enough, however, to overcome Cleveland's repugnance of Bryan and of free silver, nor was Bryan willing to seek the support of

Cleveland for his "new Democracy," which had replaced
the leadership of the Democratic party of the past.

Cleveland took no part at all in the campaign of 1900.
He did, however, predict Bryan's defeat, and the defeat of
the Democratic party in all elections as long as the party
was led by Bryan.

Subtly, Cleveland's position within the Democratic party
had changed in 1900. In 1896 the Democrats in power had
not wanted Cleveland's endorsement—they had felt that he
was a political liability, so greatly had the issue of free silver
permeated their minds that they believed the entire country was clamoring for free silver. The election of 1896 had
taught the Democratic party that free silver was not the
issue they had believed it to be, and while Bryan continued
to talk about silver, others in the party wanted to bury the
issue and talk of imperialism in 1900. Since Cleveland and
Bryan both had publicly declared against imperialism,
Democratic party leaders tried to indicate that Cleveland
supported Bryan—which angered Cleveland because that
was one thing he would never do.

It was ironical to note how highly the public and the
Democratic party regarded Cleveland's opinions, now just
four years after he had been characterized as the destroyer
of the nation by the Bryan Democrats.

Shortly after the beginning of September, 1901, President McKinley was assassinated in Buffalo, Cleveland's old
home town, and Theodore Roosevelt became President of
the United States. Roosevelt had the greatest admiration
for Cleveland, in whose shadow he had grown to political
maturity, although as a Republican Roosevelt always
stoutly opposed Cleveland policies when it was politically
proper. Cleveland, however, had lost his feeling of respect
for Roosevelt, whom he considered to be a flighty dema-

gogue. Cleveland was slow, ponderous, phlegmatic, and
not quick to find friends or enemies. Roosevelt was his
exact opposite in almost every way, and yet, when the great
coal strike of 1902 had dragged on for weeks, and 145,000
miners refused to go back into the mines, Cleveland offered
Roosevelt some advice. The coal operators were hoarding
coal, although they had a huge supply mined and processed,
in hopes that the public would put pressure on the miners
to make them go back to work. Cleveland offered some sug-
gestions in the matter, and Roosevelt, who wanted to inter-
vene, used the Cleveland letter as a wedge—a helpful wedge,
since the former President's prestige was so high with the
people of America.

When he had left the Presidency, Cleveland believed
himself to be the most unpopular man in the United States,
so deeply had the antagonism of his own party upset him.
His feelings were so strong on the subject that he declined
almost all invitations to speak or appear in public, for fear
that he would be insulted and derided.

It was true that the advocates of free silver detested
Cleveland, but as time went on the advocates of free silver
became very few indeed, and by 1902, when he appeared
on a public platform in New York City, Cleveland received
a storm of applause. After he had spoken, the crowd rushed
on the stage to congratulate and greet him. By the end of
that year many men thought Cleveland was the *most* popular man in the country, and when he appeared on a platform in St. Louis, the heart of the free silver territory, he
received an ovation that was even louder than that accorded
Cleveland's seatmate on the platform—Teddy Roosevelt.

There were several reasons for Cleveland's new popularity. One of them, of course, was that a living ex-President
is always honored, at least for a few years after his term
when the passion surrounding issues that once seemed vital

has subsided, and the former chief executive's work can be put in focus. Americans have always respected their Presidents—even when they hated their policies—for the work and physical abuse they were willing to undertake in the name of the nation.

Cleveland was honored also because every American, save the followers of William Jennings Bryan, realized that he was one of the most courageous men alive, and that in following his principle he had expressed the best tradition of the nation.

In 1904, such was Cleveland's regained reputation that he was even mentioned as a candidate for the Democratic nomination again, which pleased him very much although he had not the slightest intention of accepting or even encouraging his supporters. Having been twice defeated, Bryan was temporarily eclipsed in the Democratic convention of 1904, and the followers of Cleveland rallied behind Alton B. Parker, a New York judge, who won the nomination and control of the party. That year the Democrats honored Cleveland in the convention for having established the gold standard by securing repeal of the Sherman Silver Purchase Act, and on the convention floor the speaker was interrupted, as were dozens of speakers after him, by cries and cheers for Grover Cleveland.

Cleveland was dejected by the resounding victory of Teddy Roosevelt in the election, and he was inclined to wonder if the American people had changed—but that was the reflection of a political warhorse who never could understand what the American people saw in the ebullient T. R., and also his view was probably colored partly because Roosevelt was a Republican.

Nearly seventy, and his health now failing, Cleveland was finished with politics and public life in 1904. This election year had been a harsh year for Cleveland in many ways.

His little daughter Ruth died that winter of diphtheria, a tragic event which so upset the former President that he never again returned to the Gray Gables cottage on Buzzards Bay, because he could not bear to be reminded of the happy days the family had spent there when Ruth was alive.

In 1905 Cleveland performed his last great public service in shaping and reorganizing the Equitable Life Assurance Society—as the outcome of an outrageous insurance scandal which involved the officers of the greatest insurance companies in America who had been misusing the funds of policy holders. Cleveland brought honest and conservative management back to the Equitable and made of this great company a model for insurance management in the nation.

Even after his seventieth birthday, Cleveland made a few public appearances, although his strength continued to fail, for he suffered from heart disease and kidney disease, although the cancer taken out aboard the *Oneida* had not returned. He made a birthday address on Washington's birthday at the Union League Club in Chicago in 1907, and on March 15, his seventieth birthday, he was on his way south on a hunting trip. That day hundreds of letters and telegrams came to the house in Princeton, congratulating a beloved President on his anniversary. Even the New York *Sun,* which had battled Cleveland throughout most of his political career, published an editorial that day praising the former President for his courage and steadfast devotion to principle; and in Caldwell, New Jersey, a group of well-wishers unveiled a tablet in his name in the room in the house in which he had been born.

On the next birthday, his seventy-first, Grover Cleveland was seriously ill, suffering now from gastro-intestinal attacks as well as his other degenerative diseases. The illness became more serious in April, and on June 24, 1908 at 8:40 in the morning, Grover Cleveland died in his Prince-

ton home, as he had wished, with his wife at his side, mur-
muring his parting words:

"I have tried so hard to do right."

Two days later, the family buried Cleveland in the old
Princeton Cemetery, just at sundown. The townspeople
erected a national monument a mile away from the grave
to the reformer who had restored honesty to American
government in a time of great national crisis; who had faced
storms of depression and all but revolution in the national
economy; who had stood firm in the face of criticism from
every quarter and had maintained the principles of good
government and honest finance against strong and merci-
less enemies. He was the President who had helped the
country survive one of the most difficult, if least understood, eras of change and almost constant crisis in American
history.

At the national monument, Cleveland's memory belonged to all Americans, a memory of a strong and courageous President who had served in the great tradition of
Presidents, fighting for the right. At the grave, as he
wished, was the memorial to the man himself, a man who
had twice held the highest office the nation could bestow.
It said:

Grover Cleveland
Born Caldwell, N. J.
March 18th, 1837
Died Princeton, N. J.
June 24th, 1908

To look at the marker, one would never suspect that this
quiet bluff giant, Grover Cleveland, had ever travelled a
hundred miles from home.

✿✿ BIBLIOGRAPHY

ARMITAGE, CHARLES H. *Grover Cleveland as Buffalo Knew Him*. Buffalo: Buffalo Evening News, 1926.

BRADFORD, GAMALIEL. *American Portraits*. Boston: Houghton-Mifflin and Co., 1922.

BROOKS, NOAH. *Men of Achievement*. New York: Charles Scribner's Sons, 1895.

CLEVELAND, GROVER. *Presidential Problems*. New York: The Century Co., 1904.

FORD, HENRY JONES. *The Cleveland Era*. New Haven: Yale University Press, 1921.

FUNK AND WAGNALLS (eds.). *Builders of America*. New York: Funk and Wagnalls, 1960.

FUNK AND WAGNALLS (eds.). *Grover Cleveland Who Put Independent Thinking into Party Politics*. New York: Funk and Wagnalls, 1931.

GILDER, RICHARD WATSON. *Grover Cleveland. A Record of Friendship*. New York: The Century Co., 1910.

GOODRICH, FREDERICK E. *Life and Public Services of Grover Cleveland*. Brooklyn: J. J. McCormack, 1888.

HOYT, EDWIN P. *Jumbos and Jackasses: A Popular History of the Political Wars, 1860-1960*. New York: Doubleday and Co., 1960.

HOYT, EDWIN P. *Lost Statesmen*. Chicago: Reilly and Lee Co., 1961.

HUGINS, ROLAND. *Grover Cleveland. A Study in Political Courage*. Washington, D. C.: The Anchor Lee Publishing Co., 1922.

KEEN, W. W., M.D. *The Surgical Operations on President Cleveland in 1893.* Philadelphia: George W. Jacobs Co., 1917.

KING, PENDLETON. *Life and Public Services of Grover Cleveland.* New York: G. P. Putnam's Sons, 1884.

LYNCH, DENIS TILDEN. *Grover Cleveland, A Man Four-Square.* New York: Horace Liveright, Inc., 1932.

MCELROY, ROBERT. *Grover Cleveland, The Man and The Statesman.* 2 vols. New York: Harper and Bros., 1923.

MERRILL, HORACE S. *Bourbon Leader: Grover Cleveland and the Democratic Party.* Boston: Little, Brown and Co., 1957.

MORRIS, RICHARD B. *The Encyclopedia of American History.* New York: Harper and Bros., 1953.

————. *Great Presidential Decisions.* Philadelphia and New York: J. B. Lippincott Co., 1960.

NEVINS, ALLEN. *Grover Cleveland. A Study in Courage.* New York: Dodd, Mead, and Co., 1932.

PARKER, GEORGE F. *Recollections of Grover Cleveland.* New York: The Century Co., 1909.

SMITH, BESSIE WHITE. *The Romances of the Presidents.* Boston: Lothrop, Lee and Shepard, 1932.

WHITE, JAMES C. *Public Men of Today.* New York: F. Warne and Co., 1896.

WILLIAMS, JESSE LYNCH. *Mr. Cleveland, A Personal Impression.* New York: Dodd, Mead, and Co., 1909.

✣✣ INDEX

DATE DUE

MAR 9 - '64	OCT 19 '72		
MAR 2 6 '64	MAR 31 '73		
MAR 31 '64 AUG 5 '64	OCT 1 73		
MAR 17 '65	OCT 4		
MAR 19 '65	AP 8 '82		
MAY 12 '65	MAR 15 '84		
MAY 13 '65			
MAY 14 '65			
MAR 15 '66			
APR 9 '68			
May 5 FEB 24 '70			
FEB 18 '71			
FEB 14 '72			
FEB 28 '72			
MAR 13 '72			
MAR 29 '72			

GAYLORD | | | PRINTED IN U.S.A.